Marketing on Fleek

*How to Make Your Marketing
& Professional Efforts Count In A
Customer-Centric World*

By Kobi Ben Meir

Note from the author

Thank you for purchasing the book. I hope my journey will inspire you to aspire for more of your own. Remember this journey is ongoing and everchanging.

I invite you to follow me, stay updated and reach out with any subject.

LinkedIn: linkedin.com/in/kobibm

Website: www.kobibm.com

Disclaimer

The author has tried to recreate events, locales, and conversations from his memories of them. To maintain their anonymity in some instances, certain changes have been made to names of individuals and places including identifying characteristics and details such as physical properties, occupations and places of residence.

Although the author and publisher have made every effort to ensure that the information in this book was correct at press time, the author and publisher do not assume and hereby disclaim any liability to any party for any loss, damage, or disruption caused by errors or omissions, whether such errors or omissions result from negligence, accident, or any other cause.

Table of Contents

Chapter 1

How an Immigrant Came Across the Land of Opportunities

"Have the courage to follow your heart and intuition. They somehow already know what you truly want to become."

-Steve Jobs -

My name is Kobi Ben Meir aka Jacob Ben Meir and my personal motto is that if you don't have a personal mountain to climb, you might as well not exist. Years working in the technology sector and for businesses within the B2B and B2C industries, allowed me to work with business leaders and organizations that are shaping consumer relations for the better.

Of course, like any other person, I am the sum of my experiences and the influences I've had throughout my life. I was born at a time when the world was undergoing a dramatic change. The year was 1989, the apex of the '90s, a time when the Berlin Wall came down and so did the Soviet Union.

It was the best of times when it came to technology, ethnic revolutions, and culture shifts, as barriers melted, and the world started to connect across borders.

Living in Israel, my childhood was shaped in a house that advocated free speech and encouraged questions no matter how difficult. We were encouraged to explore passions that could make us the best version of ourselves. This upbringing and qualities shaped me into the person I am today.

It encouraged me to explore my potential at an early age which led me to join the software development program at my high school. It was there that I learned .Net and C# programming.

I was also part of the Israeli scouts and joined the organization as a member of the lead group that encouraged high school students to become guides and mentors for their younger classmates. This was followed by a stint in the Army followed by programming for an extra year in the Israeli Air Force.

That choice turned out to be a wise one. Instead of just serving in a programming capacity, I was chosen for a leadership program that got me into the civil high school's cadet program through the Air Force. After this, I was transferred to work as a software developer.

After leaving the Air Force, I joined an organization that provided SAP Business One implementation and development services. The creative freedom that was encouraged by the company had a large hand in my success but so did my time with the Israeli scouts. Using my own designed warehouse management system and a bespoke time-reporting system I had developed during my time in the Air Force as inspirations for a client's time-reporting system and other solutions that enhanced workflow.

Long story short, after working for a year in the company, I was offered a better position with more opportunities. I also worked for AT&T Israel, HOT, and other smaller projects that allowed me to expand my network and develop my professional skills.

All work and no play could have made me a completely different person. Fortunately, due to my upbringing, other passions made me a well-rounded, self-sufficient person. My love for photography and traveling knows no bounds but my passion for food is nothing to sneeze at either. It helps that my family has a Spanish, Greek, and Turkish background which gave as a diverse palette but we also dabble in African, Eastern European, and Asian recipes.

My cooking skills were refined in a culinary school when I was in my early 20s. It was during this time that I had enough money of my own and the time to explore my interests. I would head straight to class after work and then head home with leftovers and priceless experiences. In fact, the love of my life entered my life and my world filled with joy.

Passion does not have a shelf life after all. When we follow where the heart leads, we shape our own destiny; in doing so, we become better versions of ourselves. However, this doesn't mean one should stop doing other things. How else can we become holistic and practical individuals? That is the thought process that has also led me to launch an initiative that ended up becoming a banner for the LGBTQ community in Tel Aviv.

Known as 'Chong' or 'young person' in Hebrew, it attracted hundreds of LGBTQ youth to the party which was held every night. We used that influence later on to launch a social media project in collaboration with other party organizers. The project's aim was to spread awareness about the suicide support line in the community.

This really helped me and my partner expand our network but it also helped us realize that helping people who are on the brink of despair brings with it a sense of fulfillment that is unlike any other.

These projects opened the doors for a new job opportunity that literally changed my life i.e. as a marketing manager for an LGBTQ jewelry company. You would think that transitioning from a technical position to an aesthetic one would be impossible, but surprisingly, it was quite smooth.

Many of the leadership and producer skills that shaped me into a professional came into play at this point in my life. For one thing, it revealed that I had a penchant for marketing, branding, and business development which saw the realization of several successful ventures such as a photo shoot project, social media campaigns, a seasonal catalog as well as a mobile application initiative that profited the organization in more ways than one.

After working with the company for the better part of 4 years, I moved to the United States to manage one of its offices in Philadelphia. This proved to be beneficial for us both since I had already worked in NYC for 3 months for the same organization in the World Trade Center even before the offer came in. As soon as I got off the subway, I turned to my husband and said I had never felt more at home so the move was a no-brainer.

The move actually took an entire year because that's how long it takes to get a work visa and approval from the US embassy. But finally, on October 2014, we bid farewell to loved ones and started on a journey that neither of us was prepared for but one which we knew we could embark on together.

Arriving in Philadelphia was an eye-opening experience even though it was not my first visit to the city. We were two individuals who loved each other; between us, we had two suitcases and two dogs in a temporary apartment with only a few weeks for settling in. It was there that we remodeled and moved into our very own house but the experience was a nightmare.

Here's what happened. During the last trip, we had placed an offer on a foreclosed house even though our real estate agent advised not to because we didn't know anything about remodeling or maintaining a fixer-upper.

Dealing with the contractors was a nightmare so we had to DIY most of the work. But I am proud to reveal that we remodeled the house to our liking in time for us to move in a couple of weeks later. It was our first home in the US and we couldn't have been prouder.

That was a large part of the reason why I fell in love with Philadelphia and all that it had to offer. It's quite different from New York but it has a lot going on when it comes to culture, fun, and food. We spent 2 memorable years in the city before relocating to NYC and during that time, the jewelry company I worked for faced several financial issues and also started an investment initiative with a VC from New York.

Unfortunately, this proved to be a mistake as more and more people joined in and the intended CEO shifted the company's focus from the main product, jewelry to content instead. This ruined the core business so the strategy eventually collapsed and failed.

To recover damages and salvage its shredded reputation, the company turned its sights on a new partner in NYC, an Indian jewelry factory, and we moved to be closer to it. A year passed in Manhattan this way after which I was offered a job in an organization that was willing to sponsor my husband and me for a green card in exchange for my employment there.

This was a huge opportunity that I would've been a fool to ignore which led me to another major shift in my career. Long story short, I shifted from working on consumer-based products and developing lifestyle luxury brands to working on B2B financial products.

Was I terrified? Yes. But, I was also excited to take up this new challenge and gave it my all. It helped that the CTO of the organization was kind enough to mentor me and with his guidance. It wasn't long before a leadership position was offered to me. However, that success would not have been possible without my colleagues who kept challenging me and helped me become the leader I am today.

Surprisingly, transitioning from a B2C to a B2B product was not as major as expected. In fact, there is almost no difference between the two because they share the same principles. Both focus on a funnel at the end of which there is a business owner who has to use the product to benefit the business and take it where they want it to go. The only difference is that instead of a private consumer, you are catering to the business itself. I will be going into more detail on this distinction later on in the book.

This is far from the only business model that a business owner should follow. It is my experience that the more genuine you remain in the position you are given, the more successful you will be. That is why rather than trying to don the persona of a no-nonsense, stick-in-the-mud manager, I remain myself and use my experience to speak and work for the good of the organization.

Nowhere was this more helpful than when I was organizing team events that could boost morale and make teams gel. With my initiatives and team-building strategies, my team was able to push out the product successfully, but the work didn't end there. It flowed into the market effortlessly on the backs of a marketing and branding strategy that was developed from scratch and which is in effect to this day.

The position and the things I learned opened up more opportunities that allowed me to grow not only as a professional but also as a person. The accolades that grace my home are a testament to this.

This includes a nomination as a finalist for Marketer of the Year in 3 different award shows in NYC and London. Additionally, my campaign was also recognized with two campaign awards from IAC as the best online financial service campaign which was closely followed by an ANA B2 excellence award for lead generation in the small business category.

That didn't spell the end though. I was also nominated as a finalist in the B2B Marketing Awards in London for Marketer of the Year. The most recent awards my work received is from the AVA Digital awards and The Drum Marketing awards. This, along with my other awards, has allowed me to speak in professional conferences as a keynote speaker on several topics. But the work never stops...

This business experience was one of many that encouraged Forbes to invite me to be a part of the Forbes.com council community. The position gave me unique access to the platform and gave me the opportunity to become part of their expert initiative.

This is just the start of my journey and I have no plans of slowing down either. Currently, we are working on expanding our family which will be a whole different book. One thing is for sure. I will never stop growing and hope that the business strategies and personal accolades in this book show how you too can overcome mountains and be just as successful.

Chapter 2

Walking on the Path to Optimal Productivity

Two Roads Diverged In a Wood, And I—

I Took the One Less Traveled By,

And That Has Made All The Difference.

-The Road Not Taken by Robert Frost -

Living in an environment that encouraged self-expression, I was always encouraged to be my best self. I was always pushed to realize my own potential, develop my own interests so as to transform into an individual who is the best version of himself.

Dragging yourself through life doing something that doesn't make you leap out of bed happily in the morning is a life wasted. You may think you are being productive but what you are really doing is slogging. Human beings were designed for optimal productivity but few of us are successful at it because we are pushed into careers or tasks that our souls deny.

Learning happens best when we get out of the way of our own fears. Rather than following another person's roadmap to success, we can learn to adapt and take care of ourselves just as successfully by following our own inclinations.

By experimenting, we allow our natural abilities to manifest but for that to be possible, you have to embrace failure and learn from mistakes. That is how we learn to adapt and take care of ourselves, thus becoming holistic human beings that can take on almost any challenge that we are faced with.

Change From the Inside Out

Throughout the years, life has taught me a valuable lesson in this regard – **self-care is the best way to lead a productive life!** That is the only way you can work smarter not harder, fall in love with your passions every day, and make a decent living all at the same time.

This is where self-care comes into the picture. We aren't just talking about spa days and long bubble baths. It can be defined as any action you take that can help you connect with yourself. It's about giving yourself exactly what you need to become not only the best version of yourself but also feel content and be productive.

The first thing you need to do is to make this massive change is becoming more aware of your current actions and the thoughts that fuel them. Determine patterns and behaviors that you can change or improve and list them down. That way, the next time you have the opportunity to change behavior rather than going into autopilot and procrastinating, you will make an active effort to improve it.

During the process, ask yourself a couple of questions that can bring potential issues into focus. Here are some that can give you a good start:

- How many times do you say 'yes' to people even if it means sacrificing your interests?
- How many times do you check social media or your email during work?
- Do you respond to each and every correspondence without delay even if it isn't urgent?

- Do you allow people to talk over you?
- Do you have a system to manage your workload or do you just grab anything that seems important and start working on it?
- Do you get hung up on the details and refuse to make compromises?
- Do you often underestimate the time and energy needed to complete tasks?
- Do you spend more time procrastinating and less time working?
- Do you tend to overthink and thus make things more complicated than they actually are?
- Do you take risks?

You will be shocked by the answers you come up with but the good news is that these can shed light on aspects of your personality and work ethic that should be corrected.

For example, if you realize that people tend to talk over you, you will take responsibility for that negative pattern and become more assertive. Similarly, if you realize that you can take care of a lot of things by being organized, you can see your goals more clearly and start working towards them instead of slogging at a job that you don't even like!

The thing is what most people don't realize is that we get in the way of our own development because we entertain judgments and worries that are someone else's problems. We entertain preconceptions about what we should be doing rather than what we ought to be doing and that diverts us from a path of self-fulfillment to one that ensures a gratifying life rather than a boring one.

Do you really want to spend the rest of your days just going through the days? If you answered "yes," your dreams are turning to ash on that backburner as you live someone else's dreams. So how can you turn off that commentary and keep your focus on your personal productivity? By ignoring the emotional static that prejudgments and misconceptions can trigger.

This happens when we attribute the anxiety and frustration we feel in our own 'inadequacies' to our present circumstances instead of in productive activities that can actually pull us out of that depressing quagmire.

In other words, we allow those feelings to make us unproductive. After all, if we allow ourselves to get caught up in the play-by-play commentary that is other people's opinion of us, we stop being effective. As soon as we refocus, we immediately become more efficient and find our flow.

This is important because efficiency never happens in a vacuum. While we are responsible for lighting the spark, our flow arises from engagement in the tasks at hand. In other words, we are either fully involved or preoccupied with commentary.

When we are in the former state of mind, we remain distracted by negative self-talk which keeps creativity at bay even though it's right within reach. However, when we are in the latter state of mind, we work out the stiff cogs in our heads and oil them to keep moving. In other words, we get better at playing which improves productivity and when we slow down, it decreases and eventually declines.

It's about changing your perspective and realizing you are more than what other people think you should be or do.

Think of a time when you learned something new by sheer perseverance. It can be anything from passing a driving test to learning a new language or playing the piano. It was far from easy wasn't it but did you give up? No, you kept at it by overcoming the challenges as they came one by one till you finally found your groove and accomplished your goal.

Now think of a time when you clung onto something for dear life even though you knew deep down it was only harming you. It could be a relationship that went sour or a job that did nothing for you except for paying the bills. Rather than making a clean break you dragged your feet because of stubbornness or because you didn't want others thinking you were a quitter.

Here's the thing: this is delusional thinking. Having a positive outlook and realizing you deserve better doesn't mean denying the difficulties that come with challenges – it's about accepting them rather than denying their existence. That is the best way to move forward towards resolutions by taking productive action.

Don't make the mistake of thinking that by procrastinating you are keeping anxiety at bay. The more you delay, the bigger that monster gets in your hand till it comes crashing down on you when it is too late to meet deadlines. By responding to difficult tasks in a constructive manner, you can compartmentalize it into workable chunks and knock each one out of the park one at a time till you are done.

Yes, you will face difficulties during the journey but once you realize that your situations are not unique, you will find your groove and realize your goals one challenge at a time. The fastest way you can do that while still remaining productive is by letting go of things that have nothing to do with your work or which trigger negative thoughts.

Declutter Your Mind Attic

To borrow a quote from Sherlock Holmes, our mind is an empty attic and it should be stocked with items that we actually need. A skilled worker will only take tools in there that help him with his work and each of those will be organized. He knows that that room has solid walls that won't distend to accommodate clutter.

So, if we dump things or information in our head we don't really need, we will forget critical information that can otherwise help us maintain our productivity. Therefore, it is highly important that we don't allow useless information in our brain, which can elbow out useful ones.

After all, no matter how deep our memory bank is, it will be underutilized unless we know how and what to apply in particular situations. Knowing the difference between what to use and what should be ignored, the difference between the grain and chaff is the fundamental skills of a good decision-maker.

You see, when you are making a decision, you have to silence distracter or anything that is irrelevant and can influence your judgment as well. These can be anything from personal bias, current emotional state, experiences, and other factors that can distort perception. For example, say you want to declutter your home. Each time you start, you end up hoarding more stuff than throwing them out.

Why does that happen? It happens because of your failure to prioritize items. It happens because you are emotionally attached to things that you have no use for anymore. That's why you can't separate the useful from the useless to the point that you lose the latter in some dark corner.

The good news is that we can change that headspace once we realize that we are in charge of what we put in it. You can compartmentalize your thoughts to make them easier to access and identify. Think of it as moving house; imagine yourself pulling out useful information, placing them in marked boxed and clearing space to put them in.

In other words, imagine your memory changing to accommodate useful information that can help you make informed decisions. Realize that our mind is constantly in flux. When you return to your mind attic, some things may have shifted but you won't have to look long to locate them if they are compartmentalized.

Keep Your Mind On The Game And Off The Commentary

However, Holmes had only his mind. Today, we have Google and Wikipedia and social media to remember things for us. The fact is that our memories cannot possibly hold a massive amount of knowledge that we have access to now. If we allow ourselves to be buried in that avalanche of extraneous data, we will remain a product of the times and not our own selves.

For example, can you buy anything without reading reviews? Why can't you just purchase it because you liked it when you saw it? The more reviews you read, the more confused you will get. The result? You end up buying something that you regret because you thought it was the best decision based on someone else's opinion.

Similarly, when you are at work, does your mind go back to arguments you had with your partner and other issues that have no place in the workplace? Plus, when you get home, do you make a beeline to your home office to check emails from work? In other words, rather than keeping the two halves of your life separate, you are allowing them to encroach on each other because your attic is unorganized.

The key to maintaining control over that attic space is allowing your intentions to guide you. Allow yourself to notice how engaging in life, in the present, feels like and block information that isn't important. That way, you can give your brain some much-needed rest, you will know where you can find the information you need as you need it and give your work as well as your family your undivided attention.

If you wait, you quit by default. While you may be tempted to put off difficult short and long term goals for later, doing so will keep putting them off indefinitely. So if you receive an important email that requires a long reply, take care of it immediately while you are at work and when it's time to help your kids with their homework, put your laptop away and give them your full attention.

With time, you will find yourself with more time for your family and enough time for your work without ignoring either. You will also have more time to get more rest and not just for your beauty. With a solid 7 to 8 hours of sleep each day, you can knock your productivity goals out of the park one at a time.

Yes, it can be overwhelming at first, especially when you hit hurdles, but there are certain tips that can help you maintain your flow. For example, you can take care of low priority goals such as breakfast first, reduce work meetings to 90 minutes or even 30 minutes, let each team member know what you expect from them a day before so that they are well into a project by the time you show up, etc.

Plus, keep checking in with yourself to see what's working for you and what isn't. Do this every week or month, depending on your schedule and the extent of your goals to ensure you are headed in the right direction. Focus on what you can control and have a plan for the rest, but don't be afraid of making changes as you progress.

To increase your chances of success by understanding that there are some factors that you can control and some that are out of your hands. For example, while you cannot force the other departments to work faster at the last minute, you should have a plan in place that helps you coordinate the month-end close already. Plus, you can keep sending them emails to remind them of deadlines and an accountability agreement in case they fail to deliver.

Similarly, you can remain productive in regards to your career by maintaining a running list of your accomplishments on a simple Word document or an Excel sheet. This can be anything from meeting difficult deadlines to stepping in to help with an urgent project to successful investor pitches or bringing your organization back from financial ruin.

That is much better than thinking of the successes you had after a full year of accomplishments! You may miss out on critical ones that can influence the next employer you want to work for. Plus, it will also open your eyes to the skills and habits that need to be developed further, which in turn will set you up for faster career progression.

Yes, you will make mistakes, and yes, you may find yourself going back to square one more often than you will ever admit. But once you realize that failure is part of the process, you will brush yourself off and keep moving forward without sweating minor setbacks.

Eventually, you will find yourself emerging from your shell and become a better version of yourself as you tackle new challenges and gain new perspectives. Start by promising yourself that you will make this year more productive than the last and re-wire your brain to overcome obstacles. The key is to eliminate mental roadblocks that prevent you from realizing your full potential. Once you get the ball rolling, that heckler inside your head will have a hard time keeping up.

Chapter 3

Creating a Healthy Work Culture at Your Workplace

"Being a great place to work is the difference between being a good company and a great company."

— Brian Kristofek, President and CEO, Upshot

So you are more proactive now and finally have the confidence to take the next big step. What better way to do that than by climbing the corporate ladder? As a manager, you will not only have the chance to prove yourself as a leader but also pave the way towards better opportunities.

However, if your team doesn't respect or like you for that matter, do you really think they will be behind you 100%? What if the workplace culture is so cloying that it leaves no room for creative freedom and stunts productivity?

In either case, the result will be soulless employees who only clock in for the paycheck and cannot wait to clock out at the end of the day.

So how can you get the most out of them and still motivate them to come to work each day with a spring in their step? By working on your team management skills and by realizing that even though they are your subordinates, without their help and skills, you can get nothing done! In other words, you need to empower them if you want to motivate them into working hard.

The Importance of A Positive Work Culture

Before we get into that, let's establish what we mean when we say 'work culture.' It refers to the environment that is based on company values, and it creates a standard that every employee has to follow. Most senior professionals and managers believe it revolves around a company's brand value and the compensation paid to employees.

Since their priority is the bottom line and business growth, perhaps this narrow-minded perspective can be forgiven. However, as a manager, you cannot afford that outlook. You have to understand that work culture is an intangible ecosystem that can either provide a positive/productive ambiance or leech energy from anyone who has to work in it.

Only an organization and management that values human resources treats employees with respect, trusts them to perform at their best, empowers them to do better, and instills confidence can work with motivated employees. They don't work in a vacuum, even if it seems like it. Even those who come to work depressed each day do so knowing that they are working in a company that has a distinct personality.

Contrary to popular belief, a raise or positive appraisals can only go so far. At the end of the day, when a collective effort is required to bail the company out from a tight spot or meet harsh deadlines, only employees who have genuine affection for their workplace step up.

Those are the ones who have a sense of loyalty that is deep enough that they can cancel appointments or work overtime just to get work done. They are also the ones who recommend other skilled employees to give their best because they are genuinely interested in making the company grow.

What makes this unique is that it is completely organic and cannot be faked. Even an overly enthusiastic worker will run out of steam if he/she is not fueled by positive reinforcement or see their efforts ignored.

So how can you get the most out of them? First thing's first – you need to leave pride at the door. Yes, you worked really hard to get to the position you are now, but if you project that arrogance on your subordinates, you will not get anywhere.

Here are some ways you can become a positive role model who can motivate them to focus on their work rather than the hours:

Level the Playing Field

What with everything you have on your plate, it can be hard to remember what Steve told you about his son's surgery or how Jan's sprained ankle is healing up. These may look like little things, but by following up on them, you can boost flagging spirits and make employees feel special at the same time.

No one likes coming to work when they are troubled, and the only reason they do so is that they have to make a living. Remind them that their efforts are appreciated by asking about them and their families.

Connect with them on a personal level by equating their family life with your own. Jack's wife is about to have a baby? Tell him what you went through and how you share his elation. Megan's mom is in the hospital? Give her time off work to tend to her and ask about progress. Even checking up on an employee who has been feeling down can go a long way in boosting morale.

Fake it, and they will sniff it from a mile away. Genuine concern for an employee's well being and which is not tied to their work can give you valuable insight that can help you motivate them.

So why are we so hung up on motivation? By itself, it is the force that encourages people to exert high levels of effort willingly, and that cannot be bought. It can only be inspired. Consistent communication can help you level the playing field by making yourself more approachable.

Appreciate Effort

Recognizing efforts in the workplace is not a sign of weakness. It proves that you are a manager who values hard work and appreciates it. In fact, it is actually tied to job satisfaction. This doesn't mean you should thank only those who take their work home with them.

Your job should be to show each one the measurable impact their efforts have on the business in general and for the team in particular.

The fact is that leaders who appreciate are the ones who get appreciated. When employees know that their work contributes to a cause and is noticed by higher up on the corporate ladder, they feel a deeper connection with their team leads.

Needless to say, those who feel appreciated this way stick around for years that can turn into decades with consistent motivation. Even a friendly pat on the back for a job done well, or an appreciative email can go a long way in boosting morale.

These may seem like little things but they will empower your teammates to do better, drive self-action, and ensure employees come to work happy.

Create an Inclusive and Diverse Work Environment

Diversity is the spice of life, and while this quote has been used to exhaustion, it has a visible impact on today's work culture. As gender and race are now playing a huge role in hiring practices, companies are changing policies to accommodate people from all walks of life.

Unfortunately, most companies stop there. A diverse work culture can provide rich skill set and perspectives to an organization that can allow it to take advantage of hidden markets. This is where inclusion should come into the equation but is often ignored when hiring policies are met.

If you are a team lead in such a company, this is your chance to make your team more inclusive. Your job is to utilize the power of differences to encourage decisions that can result in better solutions. For example, if an employee has to get off work because of a religious holiday, give them a day off, and extend the same courtesy to the others. Similarly, if two team members are at odds with one another, make them work together on projects where they have no choice but to set aside differences. By encouraging them to understand those differences, you can empower your team to take action even when you are not there to supervise.

This will work out for you because a diverse team that works in an inclusive environment is adaptable, innovative, and can attract more talent.

Provide Exclusive Workplace Benefits

If your workforce is mostly made of millennials, the need for flexible work hours and the environment cannot be ignored. While this generation can benefit your business with innovative ideas, they can only do so if they are allowed to be creative.

However, those juices may not flow in a strict 9-to-5 environment that focuses on work hours rather than results. To prevent that from happening, you can discuss a work schedule that works for them and even allow them to work from home if they can give you the results they promise. As a perk, this can go a long way in improving company morale and attract equally innovative candidates for new job positions as your business expands.

Google is known for its over-the-top employee benefits that include meals made by in-house chefs, chair massages, yoga classes, and haircuts! While these have done wonders for its employee retention, most companies cannot afford them for their own staff. However, as a manager, you are in the perfect spot to introduce perks that can keep them motivated to continue.

This can be anything from extended vacations, unlimited PTO, healthcare, dental care, or even paternal leave. Sick and casual leaves can only benefit them so far. A paid-time-off program can not only give them sufficient time to recharge their batteries, but it will also boost productivity.

Start with giving employees unlimited PTO plans with their manager's approval, no questions asked. The idea is simple – they can take as many days off as they need as long as they get the job done.

This way they will take fewer days off since they will have more freedom with their vacation days. It will change the focus from the hours and extra hours they put into the results they get with their efforts. In other words, if you treat them like adults, they will behave like adults.

If PTO plans are not an option, you still have plenty of options to empower and motivate employees. For example, you can give flexible work hours that can work for single parents who have to attend PTA meetings or college students who are paying for their tuition with the job. If your team includes independent and free-thinking millennials, motivate them by allowing them to work from home and encourage them to share ideas.

Similarly, by offering health, dental, and vision care, you can make your team more appreciative, especially when they realize how much money they are saving. Offer this along with the extended vacations and flexible work culture, and you can create a benefits package that is irresistible and improves productivity at the same time.

Take the Sting Out Of Employee Discipline

Of course, encouragement and benefits can only take you so far if you have unruly or uncooperative employees to deal with. Make sure that you get team workers who have a good work ethic and are self-motivated. However, even HR cannot predict this with 100% accuracy. In other words, be ready to deal with some bad apples without compromising your dignity or breaking team morale.

This is important because, as a manager, you will be expected to act according to your situation. Firing someone just because they talked back to you, missed a deadline, or came in late once will do nothing but put you in a bad light. It won't be long before other employees follow suit and follow that one out the door as well.

The key is to realize that if you retaliate, you will only add fuel to the fire. Your job is to react in a positive and constructive manner that not only saves the company from liabilities but also gives the employee a chance to correct their behavior or work performance.

To do this, you will need to realize two things:

By involving the employee in the resolution process, you can come up with solutions that both of you can work with.

Almost all employees are responsible adults until proven otherwise. If a problem arises, bring it to their attention first and ask them how they can solve it.

The first thing you need to do is describe the problem you are having with them and the negative impact it's having. This may give the employee-in-question a wakeup call, and they will voluntarily offer information.

This may take some time, especially if you are facing an introvert. However, at this point, patience is key. By repeatedly asking them questions about their behavior, whether it has anything to do with their personal life or whether it has something to do with the work they are doing, you can gradually encourage them to reveal the root cause.

This counseling approach is vastly different from traditional discipline systems, which placed all the blame on employees rather than the circumstances surrounding them. The latter focuses on an evidence-based approach that points fingers and ends in resentment and anger.

The former, on the other hand, depends on two-way communication that encourages them to commit to changing their behavior and enhances their performance at the same time.

Think of it this way. Just because an apple fell way too far from the tree doesn't mean it cannot grow roots of its own. All it needs is some nurturing and understanding to grow and become just as strong as the rest.

Of course, this doesn't mean you should become a walking doormat. Employees who fail to correct their behavior despite several warnings and meetings should be terminated. This should be done if not for the sake of the business, then at least for the rest of the team's sake.

For example, would you really want to keep someone around, who encourages others to be tardy or is inefficient at their job? What about a team member who bullies or harasses his/her colleagues? Both are examples of hostile behavior that should either be nipped in the bud or eliminated with a termination.

The bottom line is your actions set the tone for the work culture of the company you work for. Don't fall victim to the traditional paradigm that discourages staff from coming forward and which is dependent on preconceived cookie-cutter ideas of what the ideal employee looks like.

If you want to improve morale, you need to abandon grandiose impressions about your own skills and show your team that you understand where they are coming from. If that means introducing benefits that can take them away from the office for a few weeks, so be it. You can always make up for the lost revenue when they come back well-rested and show their appreciation in their work.

Even discipline can work as a source of motivation if done right. If it is fueled by ego, your retaliatory actions will only put more fuel on the fire. However, if they are based on progress, you can actually end up saving an employee with untapped potential. If all goes well, you will get a grateful and loyal worker who can become assets for the company. If not, you will get a job opening where you can place a team member of your choice.

The aim is to remain positive despite the trials you go through and the team members you have to work with. By focusing on individual growth, you can create a strong group that will have your back through projects that go belly up without balking at the first short deadline.

Chapter 4

Getting Around the Marketing World

As someone who has experience in both B2B and B2C organizational models, I know that understanding customers from a personal point of view can give you in-depth insights into their psyche and needs.

From a marketing point of view, that data is a goldmine that can fuel online and offline advertising efforts, help accounting managers to determine budgets accurately, and create a dynamic work environment with a dedicated marketing team.

Of course, your marketing strategies are only as good as your understanding of current trends, news, and technology; these three elements have changed the way customers interact with brands. The selling process and customer approach are far from simple now. All people had to do was enter into a specific sales and marketing funnel, make certain choices along the way (which almost everyone in the chosen demographic did), and become repeat customers.

This is understandable. Ten years ago, people only had limited websites where they could find information on the items or services they were interested in. With the advent of vlogs, influencers, and social media marketing, their choices are endless now!

Now businesses have a harder time convincing customers to stick around long enough to make a difference to their profit margins. Sales representatives are often ignored in favor of vloggers who, let's face it, actually use the products they review. In other words, before you have a chance to market your business offerings, the customer already knows all about it AND whether they should spend money on it or not.

Traditional strategies such as cold calls, email campaigns, and trade shows just don't cut it anymore. If you want your customers to see you, you have to be seen.

'Experience' is the New Brand

The fact is that today, customer-brand relationships are not only dynamic, but they are also ever-evolving, symbiotic, and more immersive than they have ever been. Even casual shoppers own brands as much as the actual owners do, and the latter know their business is nothing without active and loyal buyers. If that means they have to communicate with them directly, that is what they should do if they want to see steady sales figures.

In other words, you have to see your customers not as a single organism, but as the sum of individuals who have their own interests and share commonalities that benefit your brand. It involves emotion, expected behavior, and perceptions, i.e., organic elements that can create a multitude of customer experiences, not just one.

Of course, even if you do come up with an equation that works, the market may not fall in line as easily. Even if they love a product one day, a single negative review may make you lose thousands of loyal consumers in a single day. Similarly, if they think they are being ignored, they will switch to your competitors, who may give them the experience they are looking for.

So how do you drown out the noise and zero in on marketing strategies that can ensure a loyal clientele? The following basic principles can help you remain afloat in a consumer-centric environment whose loyalty is hard-won:

The Value Proposition - Determine the Position and Purpose of Your Brand

Position and purpose are two key elements that determine your brand's worth and will act as differentiators in competitive markets. Today's consumer engages with those that they can get behind and which touches them on a deeper level.

To determine what they are looking for, you need to care about the things that move them, their pain points, what motivates them, and what a successful product or service means to them. This is where a buyer's persona can help you. Simply put, it is a research-backed profile that determines your ideal customer, what their days are like, what are the challenges they face daily, etc.

This is divided into more personas, which are essentially the people who influence the ideal customer into making a purchasing decision or the people they consult with before buying anything. So how can you ensure that they gravitate towards your business? By making a subtle but important shift in the way you present yourself.

Do this by first addressing their pain-points or needs to understand where their concerns are coming from. Use the information you get to train your sales and customer support team to personalize their interactions with buyers, so they can empathize with their dilemmas and provide solutions accordingly.

Create a Multi-Faceted Social Media Marketing Campaign

As a marketing manager, you already have a lot on your plate, but if you think social media marketing is just another burden, you are missing out on an amazing asset! For one thing, you have a ton of options that you can advertise through, and for another, you can actually merge them to create a single digital marketing campaign that can attract new customers and keep existing ones engaged at the same time.

The fact is that social media has changed the way we market exponentially. Gone are the days when marketers had to wait for feedback about services or products from consumers who may take ages to share their experiences. Today, the end user is fully engaged and provides immediate feedback and even posts reviews on social media platforms almost the instant a new product or service is launched. If you do not have solutions in place that can collect and respond to that feedback, you can miss out on opportunities that your competitors will snatch up immediately. You can actually get such speedy results today so why shouldn't you take advantage of it? The more branches your social media campaign has, the more varied the feedback will be.

Let's use a small example to understand this. Say, you have to create a social media campaign for a non-profit animal shelter that is trying to encourage people to adopt and donate. Say the client also wants you to reach out to the community to increase awareness about the condition and influence some of the local decision-makers to create a buzz as well.

This requires a multi-faceted strategy that can attract visitors to the shelter to increase the chances of adoptions and increase awareness about the plight of the animals. Here is how you can use social media to ensure these results:

Use Instagram to post pictures of adoptable animals at the shelter, complete with their names, history, and personalities. Share new pictures of new animals that come into the shelter regularly, so people know they have options. This includes testimonials and before/after images of pets that found their 'forever homes' to give the posts an emotional touch.

Use Facebook to create or promote an existing page that the animal shelter has by posting updates, pictures, and details about improvements made in the shelter, how the animals are taken care of, the history and experience of the staff, and special events. If the shelter needs volunteers, post about it to attract recruits.

Use Twitter to tweet about special events, share local news coverage about the shelter, referrals from people who adopted from the shelter, details about adoption days, and reminders that they take donations in the form of cash and pet supplies.

This is a basic example, but it shows what a powerful multi-faceted social media campaign can do for a service business. The key is to use the combined power of a specific audience or demographic to benefit from opportunities that each network offers.

Measure Digital Marketing Metrics Religiously

Even if you have a great social media marketing campaign, your target customers have to have access to a platform that connects them all. This is where the website comes into play, which is where they can make purchases, donations, and get answers to questions they have about the business or service.

But, is the website robust enough to ensure they can do all of that without putting them off? If no, you will lose site visitors, a fact that is pretty much a death sentence for a growing web presence. The good news is that you can prevent this from happening and manage your site reputation by keeping these metrics in check:

Number of Site Visits

Traffic is the lifeblood of a website. This is basically the total number of site visits received and can come from any online or offline source. Irrespective of the type of marketing campaign you are running, you need to measure how much it is contributing to the growth of that traffic to see if it is working or not.

These numbers may fluctuate from one month to the next. While small dips are common, a sharp decline can indicate gaps in your business model or marketing strategy that need to be addressed. Of course, you need to focus on not just the numbers but also the quality of the traffic your website receives.

By quality visitors, we mean those who actually make purchases from the brand and return to make more regularly. This will have a significant impact on your revenue in the long run since it will work on its own. Satisfied customers usually do not hesitate to promote a service or product that adds value to their lives. Of course, interactive experiences increase those visits and the number of quality visits at the same time.

There are several ways you can do this within the website itself. For example, you can post regular blogs on the site pertaining to your business offerings or promote a certain product. Need to sell a pair of stilettos? Feature them as the main image in a blog that details the outfits that go great with it. Want to attract more people to a bakery? Post recipes about some of the delicacies on offer and mention discounts.

Before starting, you have to understand the difference between unique visitors and site visits. 'Unique visitors' are people who visit your site multiple times in a specific time period and an individual who visits the site multiple times is only counted once during that time period. A 'visit' is a single browsing session i.e. if a visitor goes to another page within 30 minutes of the last page view. However, if they return after that time has elapsed, it is counted as a separate visit.

The point is to engage site visitors, make them return for more, and ensure that they share their experiences with others so your site can get more visitors. Eventually, those visitors will convert, which means more sales that can result in a significant return on your investments.

Bounce Rate

There are two types of site visitors – ones who visit your website and explore it and two, those who hit the back button after seeing a single page. The bounce rate is determined by the latter, i.e., people who visit the site, don't like what they see, and 'bounce back' to the site they came from.

Since each page is different, so is their bounce rate, so your home page may have a lower bounce rate than say your 'About Us' or 'Contact Us' page. This can happen if the design of your home page leaves a lot to be desired.

Even though the bounce rate is relative, it can tell you a lot about how well each page of your website is performing when it comes to providing relevant content and giving users the experience they want. So even if it is high, it isn't really a bad thing because the page might just give visitors what they want right away or in a few minutes (such as a page that has a survey or contact form that needs to be filled out).

There are a number of ways you can fix a questionable rate or increase the number of visitors on a single page.

Revenue per Visit and Average Order Value

As is evident from the name, revenue or value per visit is a metric that determines how much value you are getting from the traffic that is currently on your website. It is the amount of money generated each time someone visits our site and it is calculated by dividing the total revenue earned during a specific time period with the total number of visitors the site gets during that same time period.

So for example, if say your revenue for a single month is $8,000 and your website receives over 2,000 visitors on average during the same month, then your revenue per visit is $8,000/$2,000 or $4 per visitor.

What most small business owners don't realize is that most of the visitors their site gets at first will not convert i.e. they won't buy anything. Think of them as window shoppers who may or may not return depending on the experience they have.

This is where RPV can help you determine what is working what isn't when it comes to your overall sales efforts and it can also help you determine how much you can afford to spend on each customer acquisition. A positive RPV indicates that you are going in the right direction and a negative one means that your website is getting more unqualified than qualified visitors.

This can be due to anything from a broken shopping cart to a faulty Contact page that denies visitor access. So what can you do to increase RPV? Increase the number of visitors on the site and make sure that most of them make a purchase before leaving.

Besides these two solutions, you can also use average order value or AOV for a more focused approach. This tracks the average dollar amount each time a customer places an order on a website or a mobile app. To determine your business's AOV, all you need to do is divide the total revenue it received in a specific month with the number of orders it received in that same month. So for example, if you earned $25,000 in January and received 800 orders in total for that month, then your AOV for the month of January amounts to $31.

By knowing what your company's AOV is, you can come up with goals and strategies that can help you increase that value in time. Since each order you get has a transaction cost, by increasing this value, you can generate direct revenue and increase profits. Some strategies you can use for this include:

- Cross selling ("How about getting a comfy sleeping bag to go with that tent you just purchased?")
- Coupons on subsequent visits ("Get 10% off on your next visit and 30% by recommending our products to a friend.")
- Free shipping ("Pay just for the product on your first purchase.")
- Discounts on bulk purchases ("These socks cost $10 a pair but you can get one more for half the price if you buy now.")

The best way to implement the aforementioned strategies is by segmenting the customer base you have into groups. For example, segment frequent buyers into a separate group and show them targeted ads that they would appreciate such as discounts for a certain number of purchases or introduce loyalty programs that they can benefit from indefinitely.

But how do you measure this when you only collect leads rather than sell products? The answer is based on the fact that the value of anything is what it is worth to you. So if you sell a lawnmower for $2,000 on average and a lead ended in a sale, then that lead is worth the same amount of money. However, we know that most leads don't convert. If 3 out of 10 inquiries ended in sales, then that means your conversion rate is about $3/10 \times 100 = 30\%$. That means you can get $6,000 from each lead; however, since you are only closing 3 out of 10, the value of a single lead is about $6000/10 = 600.

The formula we used here is simple:

Lead Value = Value of Sale/Number of Leads

If you want to increase conversions with your leads, encourage site visitors to refer your offerings to others by implementing a referral incentives program. Determine which ones you should offer by putting yourself in your customers' shoes. Would they prefer a 10% or a 20% discount for a referral? Or would they appreciate freebies more? Should they be rewarded for referring five people, or would you get more leads if you incentivized single referrals?

Whichever model you pick, your aim should be to increase leads as well as conversions so you can do more than just break even!

Exit Rate

Not to be confused with bounce rate, exit rate is defined as the number of site users that click away from your website on a particular page whether they have visited before or not. Different pages may have different exit rates and some pages may scare away customers faster than others. For example, payment pages usually have a higher exit rate than other pages since not everyone agrees with the prices that are on there. Many customers can also change their mind and may abandon their shopping carts.

That is completely normal, but if you see high exit rates where you don't want them, you should be concerned especially if it happens to be the product page. At this point, you need to determine why people are leaving the page and what you can do to increase engagement.

For example, if say you sell swim wear online but people rarely click on them, chances are the pictures are not as high res as they should be. A viable solution in this case is replacing poor quality images with high res ones that site visitors can appreciate.

Similarly, if you sell prescription glasses online, install software that allows visitors to upload their images on the site and 'try on' the glasses without actually paying for them. Another good example is adding video content on the website that shows people using your products so site visitors can make an informed decision.

These solutions will do two things. One, they will increase site engagement via referrals and decrease the exit rate of the page at the same time.

An exit can be natural or unnatural depending on the way users leave a page. Here is a simple example that can help you understand both. Say an estate agent is running several marketing campaigns to generate website traffic for his site which has a complete form, property page and availability page.

The goal is to get visitors to fill out the lead generation form to request a call back from the agent for a property they liked. Their journey will start from the source that took them to the website, the page of the property they liked and checked for availability, the lead form they filled and hitting 'send' or 'submit' before they click away or naturally exit from the website.

An unnatural exit can happen during any point in this journey. For example, people who usually visit the 'Available Apartments' page choose the size and their budget range rather than leaving immediately. Similarly, some visitors may start filling out the form only to leave it incomplete before leaving for any reason.

The exit rate will become a problem if you don't do anything about it but the solutions are not difficult to implement. For example, the first thing you need to do is determine the type of visitor that is exiting the most and figure out how you can increase the value of the pages they are leaving from as mentioned before.

Dwell time is more important for search engines i.e. the actual time a visitor spends on a web page and in some cases, exit and bounce rate may be irrelevant. For example when a visitor scans a page thoroughly for research purposes and then exits from it, that does not mean it is under performing. They may have been completing a transaction and were interrupted or may be waiting for an answer from a customer representative etc. Similarly, some people may prefer to call you directly rather than fill out the form thus increasing that page's exit rate.

The bottom line is that there are no accurate answers when it comes to determining successful website metrics. Each business and website is unique and requires targeted solutions that you can determine with surveys or a thorough analysis of your target consumers. In other words, rather than focusing on numbers, your job should be to determine the type of visitors you get, what you can do to increase their engagement with the pages on your website and how you can ensure they remain long enough to make meaningful transactions.

Chapter 5

What Does the Modern-Day Customer Want?

Today's content consumers make up some of the most powerful audiences that brands have ever experienced, and the movement is only getting bigger. Whether your target consumers know it or not, they drive a lot of content that a marketing service or department creates.

This strategy makes a lot of sense in today's digital marketing environment that has empowered audiences by allowing them to take control of conversations and the messages that are directed towards them. They also have the right, means, and inclination to research, share ideas, post reviews, and let the world know what a certain product or service did or didn't do for them. That level of involvement has changed the way brands do business and connect with audiences.

To fully understand how far advertising has come, let's explore the annals of history and particularly how it evolved to involve the consumer. Advertising really took off first in the early 1900s on the radio and on television and suddenly, people could get a personal view of new services and products.

The movement hit radios in 1922, but advertisers had their work cut out for them because direct selling was prohibited at that time. In other words, businesses were not allowed to sell anything in a non-retail environment, but that didn't stop them from trying. For example, H.M. Blackwell, the radio host, created and used his own indirect method in the 10-minute time slot that he had. He did that by describing the benefits of living a carefree life at Hawthorne Court Apartments, which was located in Queens.

Personalization of ads took on unique proportions in the 1930s when Rosser Reeves of Ted Bates & Company introduced unique selling propositions or USPs, which describes how a business can solve a customer's problem. This was the turning point for personalized advertisement as we know it and which pretty much laid the foundation for social media marketing today.

The premise was simple. An ad should be highly personalized to the customer to make a brand stand out among others that are offering the same thing. In his bestselling book, Reality in Advertising, he described this industry-changing concept in three parts:

- Each ad has to make a proposition to the consumer and outline its benefits. In other words, it should do away with fluff and over the top claims that may not have any use for the consumer.
- The proposition that is made to the consumer is one that the competition either does not or cannot offer the same consumers. In other words, the benefits that are advertised had to be unique to the brand or for a particular advertising field.
- The proposition had to be strong enough to influence millions of consumers at a time.

Although he was already practicing the idea, Reeves coined the term 'unique selling proposition' in the 1960s. Still, ironically, it was also a time when the approach started to lose its potency. During the 1960s, consumers started to tune out repetitive new ads forcing advertisers to usher in what was known as the Creative Revolution in advertising.

At that time, the emphasis shifted to winning consumers over with humor, irreverence, and irony rather than hard facts. The result was ads that were not hard selling and were more sophisticated, but Reeves's idea was not abandoned completely.

It was in the 1970s that strategy dethroned creativity as the most efficient weapon that brands and advertising agencies could yield. With television and radio saturating markets, brands started looking for means that could allow them to reach consumers directly with television being the go-to medium.

Even though the USP was still regarded as an important metric for marketing teams, it faced stiff competition from an idea that was proposed by Al Ries and Jack Trout called 'positioning.' The duo took a more scientific and fact-based approach to branding and marketing by arguing that consumers could only hold a limited number of brand associations in their minds at a time so it stands to reason that businesses should focus on occupying a specific position in the market rather than cast a wide net that may only waste resources.

In other words, companies had to create an image of their brand in the minds of their target market, not the other way around. This concept effectively became a fitting replacement for the USP during this time period and was used by powerful brands to full effect. For example, BMW's famous slogan, 'The Ultimate Driving Machine' is still lauded for its impact on the BMW customer's fancy and the fact that it is reflective of the brand's aspirations. It resonated with an entire generation in the '70s and continues to capture the imagination of BMW fans to this day.

Even though USP was down, it was not down for the count, and it made a comeback at the beginning of the '80s when 30-second television ads were shortened to 15-second spots. The change was made in an attempt to increase profits and ad efficiency by appealing to the shortening attention span of the average viewer.

One of the most famous examples of this change was the ad campaign for the Energizer Bunny, which described the USP of the brand (longer-lasting batteries) in a short period. The unique selling proposition was enforced with a creative twist. The original ads spoofed ones that were made for other products with the pink bunny interrupting broadcast each time by refusing to stop.

However, advertising really came into its own with the advent of the internet in the '90s, but the revolution took some time to take hold. In the early 1990s, content marketing did not deviate much from traditional marketing models. If someone wanted to get their brand message to the masses, they had to place an ad on the TV, billboards, the newspaper, or the radio.

Brochures were the go-to medium for this because they were eye-catching when they were printed in color. Some companies went all out by paying for and broadcasting sponsored television programs to advertise their wares. However, these shows were not always a success, and there was no way to determine their success rate before they were aired either.

A good example of this is Microsoft's cyber sitcom that starred a young Jennifer Aniston in a television program that was bizarre, to say the least. This is how the video was introduced in an ad, "They'll be taking you on an adventure in computing that takes place in the office of Microsoft Chairman Bill Gates…..along the way they will meet a wacky bunch of 'propeller heads' and will be introduced to the top 25 features of Windows 95."

It did not take long for this marketing tool to fail.

So what about the internet? Didn't it evolve in the '90s as our parents love to remind us? Yes and no. While it had been around since the '80s, the internet didn't begin to evolve as a marketing tool until 1994. That was the time when Yahoo! and Netscape were launched. While search engines were nothing new, Yahoo! alone managed to attract a million users in a year of its launch.

In fact, between 1994 and 1996, the number of internet users quadrupled, increasing from 16 million to a whopping 70 million users. Major companies and brands took note of this and scrambled to optimize their websites to ensure they appeared at the top of search results.

That was the start of the search engine optimization (SEO) era, during which marketers started to manipulate websites to ensure they remained ahead of the pack online. Early techniques, such as keyword staging, backlinks, and excessive tagging, were the norm even though some of those techniques are frowned upon now (for a good reason). With each update of the Google algorithm, the criterion for coming out on top continued to change as it does to this day and makes marketers scramble if they want to keep up.

The aim of this algorithm is to prioritize content that users find relevant. One of the first marketing agencies that realized the importance of tailoring content to appeal to the masses was Razorfish, which specialized in SEO. The company is notable for two reasons.

The first is for their slogan 'Everything that can be digital, will be' which may sound overly simplistic today but was extremely efficient in the mid-'90s when people were splurging on fancy digital and disposable cameras. Their second claim to fame was an online art gallery that they launched called 'The Blue Dot.'

Here is what went down. In 1995, the founder of Razorfish, Craig Karaick, noticed that the latest Netscape update allowed the server to transmit data that was not requested by a user through the browser. This was called server push functionality, and Kanarick used it to create an animated logo for the online art gallery, thus creating the first animated image that was available on the internet.

This feature was incorporated later in Facebook notifications that our accounts are daily inundated ranging from weather to stock updates. These small messages can reach users, no matter where they are and what time it is, which makes them great for email. Gone are the days when users had to check into their account via their smartphones to see if they had new mail.

The process was overly long because a request had to be sent to servers which then had to search for the last email received. This naturally took time, which was quite frustrating for business owners who had to travel frequently. The process is instantaneous now so that we can access, read, and reply to emails as soon as we receive them. It made email marketing a lot easier by allowing marketers to send deals and introduce new products almost as soon as they were launched.

However, perhaps the most important entity that had and still has a profound effect on consumers and digital marketing is Google. Even though it was not the first-ever search engine made, it was crucial in changing the path consumers took to make purchasing decisions and conduct research.

It started as a concept by two college students in 1996 who named the algorithm 'BackRub.' While other search engines collected and retrieved URLs and titles according to specific keywords, BackRub used citations to generate valuable and targeted search results. In other words, it gave pages value by the number of times they were named or linked across the World Wide Web, and this is how backlinking was born. Pages that had a lot of these links were ranked higher than others because the founders assumed that if a page was mentioned multiple times, it meant that it was important to readers. This concept is in play today because Google still prioritizes this effect when it is ranking sites.

The road was far from easy. It wasn't long before people started to create huge sites that only had one function – to link to other sites and increase their rank or value. Google started cracking down on these in 2003, and it has set hefty penalties for site owners who are caught doing this.

So what did people do? They started to stuff sites with ad-heavy and overly promotional content in a bid to attract more consumers, at least till the Panda algorithm was put in place in 2011. That's because the team at Google realized that ad-heavy and low-quality content did nothing but result in unfriendly user experience.

Google got right what its predecessors never did – the user and by default, the online consumer. That's why it keeps changing the algorithm and why it has become an integral part of digital marketing. It proves its dedication to the user in its mission statement, "to organize the world's information and make it universally accessible and useful." The premise is simple – consumers have more access to data that can help them make informed decisions.

A good example of this includes online reviews that were non-existent back in the day. If someone hated a restaurant's food or did not care for the service, they had no one to complain to but their relatives and friends. Similarly, if they liked a service, it rarely resulted in more business.

Now, we can post both negative and positive reviews on Google Places and other platforms that are vying for the search engine as well. This includes bloggers who are quick to review and post their views on channels that have made them millions in revenue.

That was not the end of its offerings. In 2015, the search engine giant announced that it was introducing machine learning into its algorithm. In other words, it won't just read the words that a user searches for - it also determines the meaning of those words when they are typed in by using context.

While this is second nature to us, computers can't understand it. For example, if we start talking about how oil is destroying the ecosystem with a friend, he/she will understand that we are talking about the harmful effects of crude oil. A computer may not be able to make that connection and may think we are talking about cooking oil and how it affects our health. In other words, it will fail to understand our intent something which the search engine is still trying to perfect.

At the same time, mobile marketing was taking off as the next best marketing tool and marketers were quick to jump on the bandwagon. To understand how that happened, we need to go back a few years in 1992 when a test engineer from the UK sent the first-ever SMS message from a computer to a mobile phone which simply stated 'Merry Christmas.'

Four years later, the first mobile phone that was capable of browsing the internet hit the market and today, it is the go-to platform for business owners who want to personalize their engagement with consumers.

SMS was not adopted as a serious marketing tool until the year 2000 when marketers realized how non-invasive it was. Small and large companies started to send customers loyalty offers and exclusive deals via simple messages straight to their mobile devices.

However, nothing gave them intimate access to consumers more than smartphones which were invented at a time when traditional media was failing to capture consumer attention. However, the full impact of the device would not be realized until the introduction of the iPhone in 2007 and its OS.

Even though it was not the first smartphone, the technology that worked behind the iPhone changed mobile user behavior. That's because unlike its predecessors, such as the Blackberry, it offered productive as well as entertainment tools to its consumers.

However, the first mobile ads that were introduced on the smartphone were clunky and annoying because they were repurposed from desktop browser ads. That resulted in the need for mobile-friendly ads that users didn't have to zoom in on or squint at to understand while they were browsing through their phone.

This also resulted in app stores that allowed users to abandon web browsing in favor of mobile apps that provided instant access to services, information, games, products, and anything else a business might offer.

So instead of Googling, 'slingshot games' you can just download the Angry Birds app from the app store. The difference is that you don't have to type in the keywords in a search engine, scroll through results, and click on a link, access your account and then play. The app eliminates several steps and allows users to play instantly for instant gratification – something which marketers salivate over.

Attracting the Modern Day Consumer with Context Marketing

So, what did that history lesson have to do with the modern-day consumer? It tracked their evolution and why they prefer personalized experiences over static ones. It also told us that they conduct massive amounts of research and come to a brand with an educated outlook rather than an oblivious one.

The challenge is simple – today, both B2B and B2C marketers have to market directly but also indirectly to consumers if they want to be taken seriously. The best way to do that is to determine the target market so you know where you can start and where you need to direct your marketing strategies. In other words, you need to update your marketing with contextual solutions to attract organic leads.

This is called 'context marketing' and it is important for two reasons:

1. It allows you to create and distribute relevant marketing content that is targeted towards consumer needs. In other words, you can create content that they can practically use and will have no qualms about sharing.

2. You can market at a consumer's point-of-need, i.e. what they need what you are selling.

So, you have to create context around the relationship you have with your contacts or prospects to create content that they can appreciate and covert on. Here are some ways you can do this:

Personalized Email Content

If you want to make sure that your email campaigns hold a prime spot in each prospect's inbox, you need to segment them into hyper-specific categories. You can do that by gathering information about their gender, employment, job, income level, age, and their personal interests. The more information you can get, the more options you will have for segmentation.

The easiest way to collect this information is through website forms or surveys. This will not only give you valuable demographic information but also information that you can otherwise only guess at such as beliefs, preferences and personal interests.

For example, maybe the executive you just emailed an ad for Valentine's Day offers just broke up with his girlfriend and won't appreciate it. Regular surveys that ask users to fill out their relationship status will prevent such users from hitting 'Unsubscribe'.

Smart Ads

Face it. Most consumers are fickle. They won't take two seconds to run into the arms of a competitor if you don't give them what they want or if they think they deserve better. You may not be able to read their minds, but with the element of surprise that smart ads can offer, you can make them sit up and take notice.

We are talking flash mobs, freebies to unsuspecting customers and discounts to users who share pictures with new products. It doesn't have to be overly expensive either.

Take what Oreo did during the 2013 Super Bowl Power Outage. When the lights went out, the genius marketing team just tweeted a single line, 'You can still dunk in the dark.' The ad has a significant impact and the best part, it cost the brand next to nothing and reaffirmed for consumers that Oreo was consistently current when it came to their fans and their needs.

This type of marketing is obviously more suitable for users who spend most of their time online or on their smart devices, i.e. B2C consumers. However, this market is usually aware that their interactions with a brand are being used for its own benefit. Rather than abandoning it, B2C businesses should make their ads as non-invasive as possible like Oreo did and forego sale pitches in favor of organic content.

Video Marketing

Today, video is considered to be a versatile, flexible, and wide-ranging content dissemination tool that the modern day user relies on more readily than text-based content. It fulfills their need for instant entertainment, which can result in profits for a marketing company that can hit that sweet spot.

However, to hit that spot, online videos are not only supposed to be high res, they also have to be hard-hitting emotionally. In other words, they need to appeal to viewer emotions to make them take specific actions. Of course, for that to be possible the content has to be logical as well – it has to convince them into taking a course of action that is profitable for your brand.

While creating short and impactful videos is challenging, it is possible.

The first thing you need to do is stop thinking of video content as TV. In most organizations, video content is a response to emerging trends. Creating them isn't enough. Each has to connect to a larger experience and have the ability to move audiences into your brand funnel.

We have covered how you can do this to gain exposure for B2B and B2C businesses in the next chapter.

Chapter 6

Content Development Methods to Lean Onto

So far, we have established one thing – content is and always will be KING when it comes to engaging consumers, maintaining brand loyalty, and making sure that they can access said content whenever they want it and wherever they might be. However, to ensure this today, content marketing strategies have to be transparent (read 'honest'), creative, thought provoking and educational at the same time.

The goal should be to use the publishing and publication of content to drive authentic traffic, improve lead quality and ensure your sales team can close deals fast. But is this move the right one for you at this point in time? How do you know if your existing content marketing strategy is working or just a ticking time bomb? Well, do the following signs ring a bell?:

You See Declining Numbers

The main aim of this marketing strategy is to bring qualified and organic traffic that can convert and thus increase sales. However, you should consider changing it if:

- You have fewer site visitors than before.
- Sales figures are not as healthy as they used to be.
- Page views are declining or static.
- Your overall revenue is taking a hit.
- You are losing more followers than you are gaining.
- You get traffic that does not convert.

Search Results Are Suffering

Nothing is more detrimental to a website than a low rank on search results. There can be several reasons for this. Maybe your products lack descriptions. Perhaps the layout is offensive to visitors. Or maybe you don't make updates to your blog as often as you should. Whatever the reason, if yours is slipping down, it's time to give your content marketing strategy a complete do-over.

The Website Attracts Traffic, But It Doesn't Convert

This can happen if the content on your website is confusing, difficult to read, full of grammatical errors or difficult to follow. If that is the case, the only one who is making money is the webhosting service you use. Even if your field is highly technical but your target consumers are not tech savvy, overly complex content can discourage them from making a purchase.

All of the aforementioned concerns can be solved if one, you admit that your existing strategy is not working and two, you figure out where the problem lies and fix them one content medium at a time. Here are some of the elements you should re-focus on or adopt to breathe life into declining leads and sales:

Blogging

Blogging may be an inexpensive way and efficient way to bring people over to your domain, but just because you are getting loads of traffic, doesn't mean your existing one is profitable. How you convert that traffic into leads or sales will determine whether you can pay your bills and hosting service on time or not.

So how you can revitalize an existing blog that is not making you money? Here are some tried and tested strategies that can work wonders:

Use Content Syndication for Exposure

If you want to generate awareness and traffic, content syndication can help. This strategy can reveal the best your blog has to offer to a large audience and attract shares and views.

You can do this by sharing your blogs on credible sites where you are bound to get engaged visitors especially via social media. So if you build your social media account, you can compel them to follow you for updates. Just make sure to incorporate social sharing buttons in every post to ensure they share it

Besides this you can also go for paid syndication i.e. pay a third party publisher to share your content for you. This is a good method to reach new audiences as are content curation sites such as Quora. These are great if you want to become an authority on certain topics and ideas.

Revise the Headlines

Get them right out of the gate with attention grabbing headlines! With over 2 million of these published each day, how can you make your titles stand out? By making them actionable and intriguing at the same time.

Let's consider a simple example to understand this. Say, you are in the fishing business and want to sell reels, rods and assorted gear to novice and expert fishermen. If your blog has titles like "How to Improve Your Fishing Skills" or "How To Catch A Fish The Easy Way", you will one, attract families who want to take their kids fishing during the summer months only and two, you will lose expert anglers who already know those skills.

You lose out in both cases because you will fail to attract a market that may return to your website for more gear as the seasons change. For example, an angler who only has a rod and reel combo that can catch catfish will obviously want another, lighter setup for the much smaller needlefish.

The solution is simple. Just make the headlines actionable and concise by changing them to "Improve Your Catfish Fishing Skills before Targeting the Mekong Giant" and "Why You Should Be Using Lures rather Than Live Bait for Needlefish."

See what I did there? Rather than boring readers with information they already know, the headlines lure them in (no pun intended) to actionable steps they can take to catch a particular fish.

Get the Length Right

Contrary to popular belief, a blog doesn't have to be over 3000 words to be engaging. It just has to be engaging enough to compel readers to read till the end. So what is the perfect length? There are 3 actually and each has to do with the reaction and results you are looking for.

For example, if you are selling products such as mobile accessories or eyelash extensions, shorter posts that detail each item's specifications can trigger discussions in the comment section.

These shouldn't be more than 300 words long or you may put off target readers. There is only so much you can say about D curl lashes before you run out of words! Your readers know this and will appreciate shorter posts that answer their questions about those products. If you stick to longer posts, you will add fluff i.e. unnecessary content to make up the word count. No one likes to read through that much without getting something in return!

However, this word count is not ideal if you are trying to increase your blog's rank in the long run or if you are trying to build an audience. If you want that, then you will have to write longer posts that are more research intensive.

Aim for 600 to 1,200 words that are compelling, based on research and which answer your headline in detail. For example, if you are selling lash extensions, rather than expanding on the product descriptions, cover topics around the products such as "How To Ensure Your D Curl Lashes Don't Dry Up" or if you sell contacts you can easily write a "Step by Step Guide to Cleaning Contacts for Damage Free Eyes."

However, if you want Google to take your blog seriously and rank it higher, you need to research, write and share posts that are at least 2,450 or more words in length. Yes, these may not get a lot of comments, the bounce rate may be high at first, and it may not be shared as much as the shorter ones you have, if it is authoritative it will eventually boost your site's reputation online. Of course, these posts should cover topics that people are actually searching for.

Social Media

If your business does not have a presence on social media, it may as well not exist at all. Whether you want to attract businesses or consumers directly, you need a platform that can connect you directly with consumers and help you maintain that link with organic dialogue.

In other words, a social media strategy can help you bridge the gap between consumers and your sales/marketing team. Rather than forcing the former to go through tedious customer service reps that are dependent on scripts, connect them with your brand managers for a direct, undiluted and precise account of their grievances and positive experiences. Here are some ways to personalize this engagement using these platforms:

Personalize Facebook Posts

Facebook exposure is not easy today because of the number of changes the algorithm goes through regularly. However, it is still vital to B2C brands so you have to embrace that challenge. The key to a successful Facebook post is the objective i.e. what you want that post to actually do. Do you want people to comment on it? Start a debate? Do you want to introduce a new product or service? Whatever the aim is, it shouldn't make visitors second guess the meaning.

For example, if you want visitors to click on a link that heads straight to your blog, just posting the link will not compel them to take action. Just like your post it has to be accompanied by an enticing headline that can encourage clicks.

For example, if you want them to read your blog on the best jewelry to wear in a charity ball for instance, accompany the link with, "Want to be the belle of the ball at that charity gala ball? Follow this link for a quick answer!"

This post has a clear goal that the intended reader will appreciate and it has a call to action at the end that makes it clickable. Accompany it with a high res image of pieces of the jewelry that are mentioned in the blog and you have a recipe for successful posts that can serve you well.

Tell a Story with Instagram

Facebook is great when you need to generate comment and start debates. But it can only go so far if you have a diverse range of products and services to offer and want to lengthen their experience.

Instagram Stories can help you with that. This is basically a tool that is only limited by a user's imagination. Simply put, it allows them to add videos, GIFs and images on a dedicated dashboard. After posting that content they can make edits, add drawings and words to personalize it before arranging each post as a sequence to the story they captured.

For example, if say, they want to catalogue the story of a caterpillar's journey and how it transformed into a butterfly, they can take pictures of each part of that lifecycle and piece it together to form a single tale. Adding a few words such as "Go Caterpie!" or "Caution – Caterpillar at Work" as the insect creates its chrysalis adds a personal touches to the story that pulls in viewers who cannot help but follow that journey to its end.

Businesses have been using this tool to engage with consumers ever since it came out. Take LEGO for example. The toy brand's Instagram account does a great job of creating interactive content that pulls in young visitors. Each month they share #ICYMO (In Case You Missed Out) highlights of what dedicated fans are building using their bricks and also share mini tutorials.

Similarly, the beauty brand SEPHORA engages followers by sharing tutorials/makeup tips and by sharing discounts and deals. WHOLE FOODS does one better by sharing shopper experience by encouraging customers to share their Instagram Stories and by sharing snaps of items that are to go on sale each week.

All of these brands have one thing in common that helped them capture consumer imagination – they used Instagram Stories to show the practical benefits of their offerings and left the purchasing decision to them.

The bottom line is, today's customer is already well informed of the product or service they look up. They just want that extra push to help them decide whether they should spend their hard earned cash on a brand or their competitor. Using Instagram Stories, you can catch them at this critical point in the cycle and tip the scales in your favor just by sharing meaningful stories with them.

Use Twitter to Address Complaints

The fastest way a frustrated customer can air their grievances to the world is via a simple tweet. Conversely, it also takes them that much time to share short, glowing reviews. Which one do you think spreads faster and has the most impact?

As an entrepreneur, you know that a single bad review can bring even the most robust brand to its knees if it is not addressed on time. By answering a negative tweet quickly with a solution or a discount, you can one, maintain your brand's reputation and two, control what is being discussed.

To do that you should tap into Twitter's customer service features that provide users with basic tools that cover basic practices. Using those you can:

- Display support hours so that people know when they can expect to hear back from you.
- Enable direct messages so customers can get in touch with you directly if they wish to.
- Enable the 'support' option to reassure users that your brand prioritizes customer care.

The first thing you need to create is a compelling welcome tweet that can appear under your Twitter handle. Jet Blue does this admiringly:

"Nice to tweet you. Fly with us to 100+ destinations and experience our award-winning service. For concerns that require a response, call or email."

The message welcomes tweeters, explains what the airline is capable of and encourages them to get in touch with the airline within the required character length.

However, even this welcome mat will not be enough to stave off angry customers in the long run.

But that doesn't mean a negative tweet can spell disaster for your business. If someone tweets "Your restaurant sucks!! I ordered chicken wontons an hour ago and am still waiting! #suckychinese #worstserviceever" and you take it as a personal affront, you won't do your reputation any favors.

What you can do is analyze the tweet and figure out main grievances first. What is the customer upset about and how can you fix it? For example, rather than replying "You can switch to another restaurant" or "We have reviews that say otherwise" will do nothing but exacerbate the situation and your tweet WILL be shared.

Your job is to respond to the tweet in a calm manner by understanding that there is always room for improvement. First, apologize for their negative experience and ask for details. Something like this should suffice:

"I'm so sorry for that! We are looking into this issue and will replace your order pronto!"

Once the order has been replaced, update the client in the same Twitter thread by saying their new order is on the way and end with an apology and a promise to do better. A discount voucher with the tweet will also give the customer a reason to return and refer the restaurant to others.

Make sure that this interaction is public so that the customer knows that his/her issue is being taken seriously and that the business has nothing to hide. If the situation ends on a positive note, the entire thread will act as a free and authentic ad for your business.

9 times out of 10 you can calm down an angry tweeter just by putting yourself in their shoes and remember, you are working for your customer as well as the business.

Video Marketing

How do you create a unique experience and brand messaging in a saturated B2B and B2C industry? By creating a clear strategy that incorporates a range of videos that can pique interest, make viewers yearn for more, and given them a personalized viewing experience.

The first thing you need to realize is that the line between the two business models has blurred significantly. The outline I will present can be used for both- the only difference being the type of content you can use. While you can use the following outline for a B2B business, you will have to get more personal for a B2C model.

So without further ado, here is a simple way you can measure the consumer lifecycle to create shareable and unique videos. First, you have to outline your strategy by determining every step of the engagement process:

Target

Create videos that are informative and success stories that can prove as a good starting point that is backed by social proof. These were in the form of 30 to 40 seconds commercials that captured attention-grabbing scenarios to compel viewers to watch.

Use light humor to increase the conversion rate and make the videos more engaging. Plus, ensure the message was clear and easy to understand. This can be done with a mix of 15 second and 30 second web shorts and commercials.

Visitor

Once the target visitor visits the landing page, the content they find there should be slightly more focused. This can be in the form of informative customer success stories, i.e. a behind the scenes look at how your business helped clients realize their business goals, for instance.

In other words, use customer success as an unwritten approval of your services to create credibility. The stars of the videos, i.e. your clients, should not be given a script as such and they should not be asked to mention the brand directly. They will choose to do so themselves if they are asked how a certain service or product helped them. This can result in organic, empathetic, and personal videos that can pull in viewers.

Besides these, use explainer or how-to videos to explain specific offerings and how they can provide value to consumers. The point should be to make them convert easily via easy to understand tutorial videos.

Lead

At this point, you should have the user information you were targeting. The aim is to have the lead close the deal. So, at this stage, only success, employee-related, and educational videos should be presented.

You can do this by covering employees that gave viewers a glimpse into the diverse work culture in your company. Encourage team members to provide their point of view on a topic, general subjects and to improve the brand image. By allowing your employees to take the stage, you can give millions of viewers an inside look at the business to improve their perceptions about it.

At this stage, add value by presenting informative videos on how your products work. This includes its benefits and basically the value it offers to customers. This will help you provide value beyond your scope to potential leads so make sure the message is clear and CTA (call to action) oriented to increase conversions.

New Client

This is where the long-term strategy should come into play. Videos presented at this stage should be more meaningful to the viewer such as educational videos covering financial tips, success stories, and viewers should be encouraged to share their stories as well.

Existing Client

This user will be exposed to videos that they can connect to on a personal/emotional level. Introduce new offers, products and services by showing how they add value to convert viewers.

Besides YouTube, use multiple channels to share these stories including Twitter, Facebook, Instagram, email and Google Display. The length and dimensions of the videos should differ according to network requirements. For example, in-stream ads should not be more than 15 seconds long and story feed videos can be 30 seconds long.

Direct views should not be your main focus for your video campaign. Your aim should be to gain exposure by appealing to modern viewers who are in search of engaging and personalized content.

By distributing and sharing different versions of the videos you create on select platforms, you can ensure they are viewed regularly for steady exposure. At this point, your aim should be to check the quality of the leads you get and how much they are costing you. The more focused your content is, the higher the quality of your leads will be.

While videos are the easiest for users to consume, making one that can go down easily is easier said than done. Even a simple 2 minute video ad can take months to make but that effort is worth the exposure your business will get after you launch your video campaign.

So how can you use the aforementioned video campaign outline for a B2C business? As mentioned before, while the same outline can work for both business models, for a business to consumer operation your videos will have to be more personalized. To determine how you can sell a product via meaningful content, you need to figure out your target viewers first.

For example, say you want to promote a new line of fishing reels or fishing lures your store just received and want to make a video promoting it. If the reels can withstand the weight of larger fish, your target viewer should be both novice fishermen and sports anglers who compete in fishing tournaments. Spend time gathering insight into this target market because those will help you narrow down the focus of your videos.

At this point, your job is to narrow down the buyer as much as possible by asking yourself the following questions:

- What's my target angler's day job?
- Where does he/she live? Is it near or far from large bodies of water?
- How much does my target angler make in a month? Can he/she afford this rod and reel?
- What industries do they work in?
- Do they have a stressful job that compels them to take weekday fishing or camping trips?
- Where do they like to fish and which species of fish does the area have?

The answers can help you create video content that speaks to viewers on a personal level and convinces them that their fishing trips and tournaments are incomplete without your rod and reel.

Next, determine what your target audience should take from these videos or what they can help them accomplish. So if you want to sell a particular reel and rod combo, list down all of the benefits it offers such as the type of fish it can be used to reel in, what sets it apart from other combos and how an angler can use it to increase catch rate etc.

If for example, you are targeting families with small kids, you know that heavy duty and expensive fishing rigs will not attract many leads. Since they have small children, they would prefer fishing gear that is made for small hands, can be used easily and can catch a fish or two to excite the kids. If you want to add on to that you can do so at the end. Just show a glimpse of heavier and larger gear that is perfect for mom and dad along with the kid fishing gear to add a wholesome element that no family can resist.

In other words, the content of the video should elicit a reaction from viewers that compels them to take action. Just make sure that the message is consistent till the end and it doesn't contradict itself. For example, if you create a video tutorial for a fishing rod and include information about the type of bait you use for a fish, you will confuse viewers. Chances are they will close the video as soon as the message starts to go off course. Prevent that from happening by sticking to brass tacks and focusing on the message you want to convey.

Chapter 7

The Importance of A/B Testing

So far we have learned that data is king and measuring/analyzing it is pretty much the only way a marketer can get accurate results. Unfortunately, there is no magical formula that can get you instant results online. Today, marketing outcomes are forecasted and implemented according to the data a business receives from its clients, purchases, transactions, conversions or educated assumptions.

As the preferences of the average consumer diversify, marketing teams have their work cut out for them. Assumptions and guesses usually fall way off the mark when it comes to guessing what a site visitor will do on a website and what can make them click and convert.

The first thing you need to understand and accept is that websites are part of a whole. You need hard data to understand how a specific audience will respond to particular pages and elements to determine the changes you should make.

The Importance of A/B Testing

This is where A/B testing proves invaluable. Also known as 'split' or 'bucket' testing, this experiment allows online marketers to determine how slight changes in marketing influence consumer behavior. It does this by comparing two or more versions of a single page that are displayed at random. It's a comparison test that helps marketers determine which elements they should keep and which ones they should discard for better conversions.

Before setting up an A/B test, the first thing you need to do is determine the metrics that drive your business and what a successful marketing campaign means for your company. Metrics for conversion are unique to each business. For a B2C e-commerce business, it may be product sales while a B2B tech business may prioritize quality lead generation.

With time, they can combine the results of their experiments into a winning formula and show a measurable improvement with the new experiences. Introducing small changes and measuring consumer responses over time optimizes their experience for the desired marketing outcome.

But there is a dilemma here. No matter how much data you collect about your target consumer's behavior and preferences, they only tell you about past experiences, not how they can react to new products, campaigns and web pages. So how can A/B testing reveal a future that even existing data cannot predict with accuracy?

To understand this, let's take a look at some real-life examples of organizations that used this test to optimize visitor and consumer experience:

WallMonkeys Discovered That Simple Changes in Home Page Design Make A Huge Difference

The first thing you need to do is come up with a theory of why a certain marketing element is not working. That's what WallMonkeys did, a company that sells a wide range of wall designs and decals for businesses and homes across the US. After running some tests, they determined that the home page on their e-commerce website could do more to attract more clicks and conversions.

So they focused on its design which was supposed to be efficient from a design point of view. It had a high-resolution stock image complete with a headline and simple CTA, all of which worked well with the organization's goals. They decided to take a closer look at the heat maps that showed them how users were navigating their page and where their attention was going the most.

What they found was that there was a lot of activity around the headline, logo, the CTA and the navigation bar on the website. So they decided to change the image on the website with one that was more whimsical that showed customers the experience that their products could give them. The conversion rate for the new design was more than 25% higher than the one with the original image.

The test worked because WallMonkeys made an educated guess based on data generated by heat and scroll mapping tools to determine areas of site activity that needed an update.

Electronic Arts Discovered That Baiting Gamers with Incentives Rarely Works

What makes A/B testing invaluable is that it can reveal hidden pitfalls about marketing initiatives that you may not be able to predict. That is what almost happened with Electronic Arts, a global leader in digital interactive entertainment. Tasked with releasing a new version of its super-popular SimCity franchise, the company was aiming for high sales figures from the start.

The game was already popular so why was the company concerned? Like any ambitious business, the company wanted to maximize revenue from the game as soon as it was released and from pre-sale orders. To determine this, it launched an A/B test for the different versions of its sales page.

The original or control version of the page offered a 20% discount for a future purchase for anyone who pre-ordered the game. The variation did not mention the pre-order incentive. Now, as a marketer, you would naturally assume that gamers would prefer to save money and would naturally have no qualms about pre-ordering if they could do that.

The results blew that theory out of the water. The variation (i.e. the page that did not offer the incentive) ended up outperforming the control version by about 40%. Turns out fans of the game just wanted to get it and were not interested in a discount. Half of the sales of the game were digital.

This test proved successful in terms of sales figures and it proved efficient in helping EA discover that their target consumers didn't play any other games other than SimCity. That's why the incentive did not interest them. This type of behavior is difficult to understand so it is impossible to predict unless you experiment with A/B tests.

Top Elements for A/B Testing

So which aspects can you change to create variations that can help you determine specific results? As is apparent from the aforementioned case studies, you need to devote time, energy and resources on impactful elements because you have limited time to do so. Here are some of the first testing elements that you should focus on first:

The Headline and Sub Headline

This statement has been overused to death but your headline will always be the first thing a user will focus on when they land on the website. If it does nothing for them, they will leave. You need to identify a problem and make a 5 to 100 word tagline out of it. For example, if you have an online costume jewelry store, your headline can read:

Pair Complex Outfits with Creative Jewelry Options

Then you need to come up with a sub-headline which should give your site visitors the solution to the problem:

Browse Through a Range Of Costume Bracelets, Earrings, Bangles And Rings For A Look That Is Completely YOU

Of course, this formula is not set in stone. Test different variations of the content with several AB tests and determine which one has a higher conversion rate. Does your target audience prefer a softer approach or a hard sell? Will they like incentives or should you stick with whimsical copy that triggers their imagination?

The CTAs

Your CTA or call to action tells readers what you want them to do. Needless to say, the copy has to be enticing and it can only be that if it offers them a value that they cannot resist.

In an A/B test, even changing a single word can influence your conversion rate. Similarly, changing the color of the button, its size and shape can also impact performance. However, as you can see from the aforementioned case studies, focus on one change at a time. For example, if you are changing the color of the font on the headline, don't change the color of the link in the same test.

If you implement both changes, there is no possible way of determining which one is responsible for generated results.

Content Depth

Contrary to popular belief, there is no set formula on how long a piece of content has to be to convert. The answer depends on your target consumer. For example, if you offer a web hosting service, your audience will prefer a long-form page with enough details that can help them make an informed decision.

On the other hand, if you sell products such as DSLR cameras, your target consumers will appreciate short, bulleted and concise descriptions of each one. Both options have one thing in common – they can help your visitors make an educated buying decision. However, if you switch tactics, that conversion rate will go down and fast.

A simple A/B test should be sufficient in helping you determine which version can convert the most. Just like with CTAs, you should compare and contrast different variations before settling on the best one.

Email Marketing

An A/B test on an email marketing campaign is pretty much straight forward. Just send 50 or so emails to reader A and 50 of the variation to reader B and see which ones convert the most. It has to run long enough to generate actionable data.

As mentioned before, changing even a single element can give you different results. For example, say you run an email campaign for 30 days and 10,000 people read each variation. If the original version outperforms the variation by more than 70%, you know that you have a winning formula.

Anything from different content to a change in the email design can generate valuable data. Since the same number of people will receive the emails and variations, you can filter down to a conclusion that works for you.

A/B Testing and SEO

While Google encourages and permits A/B testing and ensures it does not affect search ranking, abusing that privilege can jeopardize your website's existing rankings. To prevent that from happening, here are a few things you need to keep in mind before conducting the test:

Avoid Cloaking

Cloaking is an unethical practice that some site owners can use to try and fool search engines. They just show them different content than their visitors would see. Needless to say that if discovered, it can demote your site or get it removed from search results.

I know what you are thinking. When you perform an A/B test you are splitting traffic between two versions of a page with similar content. However, this is not a concern as such because Google penalizes similar pages that have different URLs, not the same ones your pages share.

Use rel="canonical"

If you are A/B testing with multiple URLs, you may be accused of cloaking. Prevent that from happening by using the rel="canonical" attribute to point the variations back to the original page version. This will help Google bots distinguish between the pages and deter penalties.

Use 302 Rather Than 301 Redirects

This will come in handy if you run a test that redirects the original URL to a variation. A 301 or permanent redirect will tell the search engine that the change is temporary and that the original URL should remain in the index, not the variation.

Chapter 8

Call to Action and Social Proof

One of the most meaningful forms of advertising is word-of-mouth which has as much relevance today as it did from the dawn of marketing. Think about it. If you are searching for a dog bed for instance, would you buy the first one you like online or the one your friends love and which you saw in real-time?

This is a great example of social proof which is a theory that people tend to accept the opinions and actions of people that they love and trust. In other words, we are more willing to adapt our behavior according to what our peers are thinking and doing.

Think about it. Would you rather visit a restaurant that has a line out the door or one that has empty tables to spare? Would you buy a camera that has rave reviews or one that hasn't been in the market long enough to generate them? Which one do you *think* will give you the most value for your money? The former has more appeal, doesn't it?

Of course, the type of social proof you use will depend on your industry and offerings. For example, if you are looking for recommendations for say fishing gear, the first people you ask for advice will be family and friends who are anglers themselves.

If you are looking to buy something more expensive such as the latest iPhone, you will scour reviews from experts and influencers before asking your circle of friends. Now if you can use that social proof in your call to action, you can add legitimacy to your offerings that will automatically make them valuable in the eyes of your consumers.

Top CTA Elements

So how can you do that? By focusing on the elements that make up actionable CTA buttons. These should be vehicles that can direct visitors from one piece of content to the next for conversion purposes. Here are the top elements you should be focusing on:

The Design

A blog and a website will provide different design options, but the size of the space you can work with will remain the same. To ensure your site visitors cannot miss the button, it should hold center stage. Take Overflow for instance:

The call to action contains a prominent headline that identifies the problem and a subheading that provides a solution. What makes the message pop is its simple design which takes advantage of white space as a contrast. Plus the two buttons at the bottom of the CTA compel users to take action. By making the 'Get started for free' button a vibrant red and the 'See example'

button a contrasting navy blue, the home page gets the results it is designed for.

The Message

Did you know that just by changing a pronoun in your CTA you can improve conversions? For example, just by changing 'start your free 1 day trial period' to 'start my free 1 day trial period' you can increase those numbers by about 90%. Similarly, just by changing 'Get your eBook now' to 'Download your eBook now' you can get more downloads.

These two examples have one thing in common – their message makes the user experience personal and thus, actionable. The simple language tells them what they have to do to get the book so basically, it hits two birds with one stone.

The mark of an effective CTA is the experience and journey it takes consumers on. Take Overflow's home page for instance. The call to action "User flows done right" and naturally flowing subheading "Turn your designs into playable user flow diagrams that tell a story" naturally flow into the two CTA buttons on display which gives users two options.

The first one tells them they can start for free and the second gives them an example that can help them make an informed decision. In other words, the language used is simple enough to make an instant impact and actionable at the same time.

The Placement

According to HubSpot, only 6% of leads come in from CTAs that are embedded in blog posts. This mostly has to do with the fact that most readers don't read blogs all the way through or enough to get to that critical button at the end.

To be actionable, the button has to be in the middle of the post provided that it does not interfere with the meaning of the content. For example, if you want to increase leads via guest posts, you know you cannot promote your business overtly if you want your content to be seen as an expert piece.

So what do you do to make sure that at least some readers are redirected to your e-commerce or sales page while reading the post? Simple. You use an anchor text CTA. This is a single line of text in H3 or H4 styles that make it stand out from the rest of the copy. Here is a simple example from a HubSpot blog:

As you can see the CTA offers target readers (marketers) a free 12-month marketing plan in minutes. Making the jump from free templates to a free plan that they can get in 10 minutes is simple and better yet, absolutely free. It is little wonder why more than 90% of leads come from these simple yet powerful links.

But what if the reader ignores the link and keeps reading? That is where the close cousin of the anchor text CTA, the internal link CTA comes to the rescue. This is the same as the former, but it is not isolated from the rest of the copy with a style redesign. As is apparent from the name, this CTA is embedded in the content itself so it can blend in more naturally.

Take the same blog as an example. If the reader failed to click the CTA link in the beginning, they are given multiple chances to do so throughout the blog. This includes the conclusion which ends with:

Simple Marketing Plan Template

Of course, this type of planning takes a lot of time and effort. So if you're strapped for time before the holidays, give our new Marketing Plan Generator a try. This tool simplifies yearly planning and lays your strategies, initiatives, and goals out in a simple template so you can identify what's most important for the coming year.

Try our free Marketing Plan Generator here.

As you can see, the term 'Marketing Plan Generator' was hyperlinked discreetly as a solution to a problem highlighted in the paragraph. The paragraph goes on to explain the tool and ends it with another anchor text CTA as a final stroke (of genius!).

In other words, by incorporating both internal link and anchor text CTAs in your blog copy, you can increase your conversion rate significantly. Whether your readers click away after reading halfway or reach the conclusion, you will receive results.

If you don't get the numbers you are looking for, take a good, long look at the language and placement and use A/B testing to determine which variations work. Put your anchor texts to the test by testing out keywords that your target readers may be searching for and use them in the copy. Make your job easier by experimenting on old posts that rank in the search first. This will give you a good idea about the types of keywords you should be looking for.

Chapter 9

E-Commerce Marketing

None of the aforementioned tips will work if your online store does not facilitate site visitors. Even if you have a ton of valuable products and services for sale, if your inventory is cluttered or not updated regularly, traffic will slow down to a trickle or worse.

The key to a good e-commerce website is to make searching effortless. In other words, if your visitors find themselves navigating to multiple pages just to get to the checkout page, they will abandon their cart. All of these issues can be nipped in the bud with simple and user-friendly design elements and customer friendly practices. Here are a few strategies you should consider:

Make a Great First Impression with Your Home Page

Site visitors take up to 8 seconds to form an impression of a website. That's how fast you lose paying customers if the home page leaves too much to the imagination. Unless you own a major brand, chances are your potential customers will make an impression about you from this page.

The worst thing you can do is cram information into that limited space. Yes, you are extremely proud of your offerings and want the world to know, but you have to accept the fact that they aren't huge fans (yet). The aim of this page should be to encourage them to take a deeper look and explore the website.

Here are some elements it should have:

Reduce Loading Time

Today's consumer is impatient. A cheap web hosting service may be budget friendly, but it will do nothing for your bottom line. Use a page speed tester and make sure that the mobile speed is optimized for the best results.

Use Quality Images

Use few but high quality images to peak interest without overwhelming visitors. Plus, also make sure that they are small in size (less than 500 KB).

Implement clear CTAs

People will not spend much time looking for the checkout or sign up button if it is not obvious. If the home page is simple and uncluttered their eye will go straight to the CTA.

Make the Checkout Process Easy

The biggest conversion killer for any online store is a confusing checkout process. Your aim should be to balance functionality with design for a system that can entice people to make more purchases. Here are some elements you should focus on to ensure this:

Allow Users to Edit Cart Items

Shoppers change their mind all the time. By allowing them to update or remove items from their carts, you can ensure a positive customer experience.

Allow Users to Contact Support As and When They Need To

Frustrated or confused customers don't want to wait for answers. A simple chat option on the website can do wonders for your conversion rate. In most cases, this can be done with live chat or chat bots.

Ensure Product Images Are of the Highest Quality

By high quality images we mean images that are authentic and representational. Most customers return products because they don't look like their pictures. Make sure this doesn't happen by allowing them to see a larger version of the products via a zoom function.

Consider Free Shipping without Ignoring Your Gross Margin

Most users abandon their carts if they think the shipping costs are not worth the item they are purchasing. This can happen with single purchases. After all, would you splurge for $50 in shipping costs when the item you are buying costs just $10? Consider removing it or give discounted rates to loyal customers to increase your conversion rate and referrals. Keep your gross margin in consideration by reducing orders for free shipping and by increasing the basket size.

Clarify the Returns Policy

The key to a good return policy is to prevent a return. Most people return products they are not happy with. However, they can be convinced to make purchases if they know they can get a refund or an exchange easily in case there is an issue. Here are some elements of a good policy:

Make It Easy to Find

Frustrated customers can turn to other online stores if they cannot return products easily to you.

Eliminate Hidden Return Costs

They are already unhappy with the products. If you are explicit about the costs, they may be more willing to make another purchase or consider an exchange.

Use easy to understand language – Make sure that the language used in the Return Policy is easy to understand and to follow.

Use Explicit Product Descriptions

Clear and precise product descriptions can help customers make an informed purchasing decision. Think of that content as your store's sale staff and you will understand the tone you need to use. Basically, it has to be short, to the point and detailed. For example, if you are selling a jacket online it should come with these specs:

- Available colors.
- Available sizes
- Dimensions
- Texture
- Fabric or material used

Here is a simple example of a product description from the brand Forever 21 that covers all of these aspects:

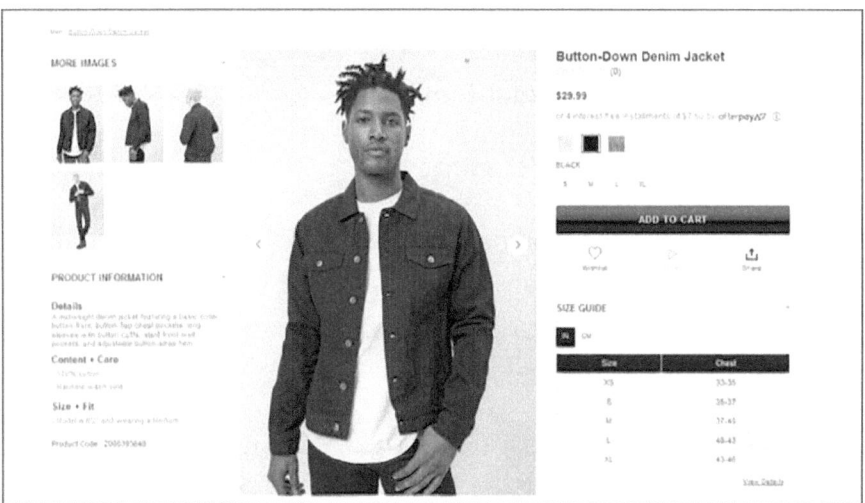

As you can see the description provides to the point details, how the jacket is to be cared for, a size guide, available colors as well as clear images. All of these small details create a snapshot for a site visitor who is exploring other options as well. The aim should be to give them just enough information that they can take in completely with a glance.

Your aim should be to capture your customer's imagination and tell a story with your product description. Will it save them time and money and make them look good? Appeal to their emotional needs and show them that their existence was bereft without it. Place the images on Google images to improve SEO and attract more customers.

Make the Content Easy To Scan

Clunky text and huge blocks of content do more harm than good for your bounce rate. Revise your existing content to be as short and to the point as possible or you will lose visitors. Here are some elements you can look into:

Break Up the Text with Headings

Headings and subheadings act as road maps for readers especially those who scan rather than read each line of content. These also act as bookmarks that users can refer to if they want to find particular information.

This is important because users don't read on the web per se. They pick out a few sentences and parts of sentences that have the information they need.

Eliminate Distractions

Get rid of or trim down overly large and flashy social share buttons that pop up in a user's face. These are only annoying and let me promise you one thing – no one will click on them if the content is not shareable or interesting enough.

The same is the case for subscribe popups that appear when the user is just a few minutes in the website. They want to read the content, not sign up yet. You need to give them time to do that or you may lose them to competitors.

Don't Fill Up Negative Space

A cluttered web page results in information overload. It also prevents users from honing in on the data they are looking for. So include white or negative space in each web page so that they don't ignore your offerings or click away.

Use Active Voice

Active voice is important for web copy readability. For one thing, it is catchy and straightforward which short attention spans can relate to. The information can also grab attention instantly and the message is easier to understand.

For instance, which one sounds better?

At XYZ our aim is to provide skincare products that can turn back the clock

OR

Our skincare line will shed years off you.

The first line takes time to come to the point but the latter does it instantly. Which one would you gravitate towards?

Use Bullets and Numbers

If you have a lot of content to share, do so by breaking it down into bullets and numbers. These provide short bursts of information that users can recall easily and break up the text layout.

Both factors work to make the content readable and easy to recall. These are particularly useful in product descriptions which users usually skim through filtering information they are looking for. Descriptions that are written in paragraphs are cumbersome. Features that are listed in bullet points are easier to digest not to mention, easier to follow.

Use Multi Step Forms

No one likes to fill out long 'Contact Us' or Signup forms which is why lengthy forms have such high abandonment rates. The aim of your form should be to encourage users to give up the minimum amount of information needed close to a conversion.

In case your website demands more than two steps, use multi step formats. Just break up the lengthy form into multiple smaller ones which can act as steps that demand a single piece of information from the user. By completing each step in the process, they can get visual feedback on how many steps are left and how far they have come in the submission process.

This works well because it offers users an interactive experience that is immersive and gives them a sense of achievement that a single form fails to do. The idea is to make them give up information willingly so what better way to do that than by making the process a brief game? The whole process will feel less time consuming and more fun.

Make the Website Mobile-Friendly

Searching for a product online takes minutes if a user has to use a laptop or PC. However, the same task takes seconds on a smartphone. Which one do you think your target customers prefer? A website that is not mobile-friendly or responsive loses customers to competitors faster than you can blink. Here are some tips that can help you convert your browser-friendly website into a mobile-friendly one:

Design Keeping Fingers in Mind

This may sound odd, but not if you think about how much time we spent scrolling through our phones and smart devices. To provide the same convenient navigation experience, make sure that your website can be navigated with only one thumb. Pinching the screen should not be necessary at all.

To determine the parameters, consider the fact that the average width of a normal index finger is about 16 to 20 mm for most adults. If you convert that into pixels, you get about 45 to 57 pixels that can allow a user's fingers to fit in the target page. Thumbs would require about 72 pixels in comparison. For this to be possible, the targets should be big enough to be easily selectable and prevent accidental taps.

These parameters will make navigation easy, makes content readable without the need for magnification. This is important because you want users to navigate your website using their phone hand without using their other hands.

Make Product Images Responsive

Your customers want to see crisp and clear images of your products when they tap them. Plus, those high res pictures have to load fast enough to prevent frustration. To fulfill both requirements, make sure that the quality images you use are cropped and resized appropriately so that they can fit on mobile screens.

A general rule of thumb is to ensure images range in size from 240 x 320 to 2560 x 1440 to fit on said screens. Here is a simple breakdown on image size according to screen size:

For small screens: 0 to 620 px.

For medium sized screens: 525 px to 807 px.

For large screens: 562 px to 825 px.

Keep Content Short and Sweet

Mobile screens are significantly smaller than a PC or laptop screen. Naturally, the content should be just as short and sweet. The thing is that the way users read on a mobile screen is different from how they scan a desktop screen.

For instance, a desktop reader is usually drawn to content on the top left part of the screen first. However, when they are gazing at their smart device, their gaze is directed to the left but it is also distributed. In other words, you must make sure ALL of the content on the page is optimized.

Start with the headline first. This should be short enough that it does not take over the mobile screen completely. At most, it should not be longer than 5 or 6 words max. It should also pique user interest by letting readers know exactly what they can expect from the content.

Of course, not everyone will be impressed enough to read on. To give them a taste of what they can expect, write a summary of the content in the first paragraph and leave the decision to read on to them.

Also use chunking to make the content easier to read and consume. Chunking means that related content should be grouped into groups or separate chunks to make reading easier. So you should be left with different portions of content that are easier to take in than large blocks of data that can overwhelm a user.

Additionally, mobile users aren't as patient as desktop users so you have to make sure that your web pages load faster on a mobile. Google recommends a 3 second long load time. Any longer than that and your site's bounce rate can increase by 90% or more!

Handle Complaints Diplomatically

The customer is not always in the right but that doesn't give you the right to be rude and dismissive. Being so can make you lose potential customers and give your brand a bad name. Resolving conflicts is rarely easy but you can make the process easier for yourself and the consumer by keeping these best practices in mind:

Allow Customers to Explain Themselves

An irate customer may seem as if they are yelling nonsense, but there are facts in their tirade you should focus on rather than your annoyance. Give them time to calm down and explain their issue so you have enough information to help them.

Apologize

Yes, you did nothing wrong and their beef is not with you, but your customer representatives represent your brand. By empathizing with customers they can calm them down and validate their concerns at the same time. Remember, their aim should be to find solutions for their complaints, not fight to see who is right. In fact, even if the customer is in the wrong, you can't go 'neener neener!' and let them have it. A simple *"I am sorry you had that experience ma'am/sir – can you please detail the issue so I can help you further?"* would suffice.

Do Not Make Unrealistic Claims and Promises

The worst thing you can do at this point is back yourself into a corner by promising solutions for a customer that cannot be kept. For example, if you say you can give them a refund when the company policy states that an exchange is preferable, you may lose face when you have to go back on your word. If there is no resolution consider how else you can help them. That's much better than raising their hopes only to dash them later.

Transfer Quickly, but Explain Why

If the complaint is not related to your department or is refers to your area of expertise, you should transfer it to the appropriate department. However, a simple "please hold while I transfer you" will do nothing but make the customer angrier.

That's because you should never miss an opportunity to explain to a customer why a proposed course of action is for their benefit. So, instead of that say, "I'm going to connect you to our specialist who will get that squared right away for you. Please hold." This will placate the customer, reassure them that their complaint is being taken seriously and ensure they remain on hold.

Follow up using supportive queries – Don't blow the entire exchange by getting passive aggressive at the end! There is fine line between following up and triggering a customer negatively. For example, look at these two responses:

"Is there anything else I can help you with?"

"Is there anything else wrong?"

The second is a negative question that can lead to an equally negative outcome since it can be misconstrued as a passive aggressive dig. Conversely, by asking them how else you can assist them, you can reassure them that all of their complaints are taken seriously.

Don't Drag Out a Lost Cause

It happens to the best web stores. No matter how polite you are, how many discounts or benefits you offer, some customers just cannot be placated. The first thing you need to realize is that those instances should not be taken personally. Winning customers over is well and good, but if one already has both feet out the door, parting ways is a better idea than dragging out an irresolvable dispute.

Customers who say they will never return or cancel their account aren't always gone for good. They can be convinced to return if the issue they couldn't forgive is resolved later or via benefits that are too tempting to resist.

Make Sure That the Ads Take Users to Relevant Pages

Your online ads will do nothing for your conversion rate if they not linked to relevant web pages especially. This includes:

The Landing Page

That is where the real conversions take place and not the home page as is the generally accepted norm. That's because your home page is just a pit stop that points to the rest of your website's content. In contrast, a landing page is a destination where you need your site visitors to end up. It's your conversion-centric machine that follows a set of design principles that focus on target customers. By creating and distributing ads that rely on visitor expectation you can join a conversation they may already be having in their head. Link those ads to a landing page with a signup sheet that can fulfill those desires and you have a recipe for ad success.

Product Pages

If you have an online retail business, your aim should naturally be to focus a site visitor's attention on the products. If that is the case make sure that your ads take visitors to specific product landing pages which are designed to incite action. If it is set up correctly (with a catchy headline or product description for example) it can pop up on search results as well.

Capture User Data on Exit

You cannot stop visitors from leaving your website, but you can capitalize on their exit by capturing essential data via exit popups. As is apparent from the name, an exit popup is a popup that appears on user's screen as they exit a website. It's basically your last ditch effort to keep a prospective customer on a page. Here are some examples you can use:

Ask For Their Email Address

A simple example is to create one that reads, "Leaving so soon? Leave your email address with us for fantastic updates about discounts and deals!" The aim is to make them want more and to ensure they leave with an intent in mind.

Ask Customers to Rate Their Shopping Experience

This popup should be in the form of a simple survey that the user can fill in seconds. For example, ask them if they found what they were looking for with a simple yes and no at the bottom they can select.

Use Dynamic Content

Improving your company's user experience is key when it comes to keeping people happy with its offerings. However, even though customer acquisition should be a priority it should not be at the expense of losing existing ones. This is where dynamic content can prove invaluable. This is basically content that changes based on user preference, data and behaviors. Here are some ways you can attract both using dynamic content:

Make Use of Site History

There is a reason why you get a list of amazing Netflix recommendations each time you log into your account. The results are based on what you watched previously and they keep changing based on future views as well. Use this concept by researching your users' browsing and purchasing histories and create content around it.

Create Personalized Emails

Using dynamic content, you can personalize almost every aspect of an email to target a particular user. This includes their gender, geographical location and purchase history. You can also customize emails depending on their last location and offer them discounts based on how long they have been your customers. A simple 'Hey (customer name)' can make the reader sit up and take notice instantly.

Make Use of Conversion Optimization

Conversion marketing is basically a system that can help you increase the number of customers you have by increasing the percentage of visitors on your website. Since each company and its goals are different from the next, this system is also unique to the business using it.

This includes exit rates, creative CTAs and bounce rates which I covered in detail in previous chapters. All of these have one thing in common though. They rely heavily on user experience. While most of the issues can be fixed with high quality web design, poorly written content can derail your efforts even if your website is a sight to behold.

Use Cross Device Matching

Cross device matching allows marketers target users across all of their devices and channels. While cookies are quite useful in tracking online desktop users on smart devices, they reset when the user closes the browser. That's because they aren't designed to work on multiple devices.

Cross device ID tech or XDID overcomes this problem but it can only work if you have a complete view of your customers. In other words, if you don't maintain dynamic customer profiles that grow with them with time (something which cookies cannot track) you will not be able to collect personally identifiable information.

XDID use two methods to determine target consumers to create relevant experiences:

Deterministic – This approach uses determined user data to match users to devices such as their social media credentials, email addresses etc.

Probabilistic – This approach makes use of anonymous data signals such as the type of browser uses, choice of OS, IP addresses etc.

Both approaches need to be explored thoroughly because they can work well together. While deterministic capitalizes on insights from specific data, probabilistic uses speculative data to map potentially accurate customer profiles.

Offer Incentives to Increase Sales

Consumers have their choice of online stores and will pick those they think offer them the best value. The best way to stand out among competitors in this case is by giving them incentives that can make their purchases worth more to them than any other company can offer. Here are some ways you can do that:

Offer Free Shipping

Most consumers will abandon their shopping carts if they think the shipping fee is not worth their purchase. This can happen if the total worth of their chosen items is less than the price to ship them. By offering free shipping to new customers, you can reduce cart abandonment rates exponentially.

Offer Free Gifts

Getting a free item with their purchase will naturally make consumers feel appreciated and valued. You can even slip free samples in their packages for a pleasant surprise.

Use Affiliate Marketing to Increase Sales

This monetizing avenue can help you make money even when you are not working on your website and business. Here are some ways you can use it to increase sales:

Promote Relevant Products

If you promote affiliate product that are not relevant to your target market and the content those links will be included in, you will only put off customers. For example, if you run a gardening blog there is no point in adding a CTA at the end for readers to buy your food supplements.

Use Sustainable SEO

Search engines are way more sophisticated today than they were just a few years ago so you cannot rely only on keyword research for your affiliate content. In other words, rather than prioritizing keyword density you need to based your content on answering queries your target consumer is asking Google.

Chapter 10

B2B Marketing

If you are selling directly to customers, you are a B2C Marketer (Business to Consumer). However, if you are into B2B Marketing (Business to Business), that means you work for a business that sells services or products to other organizations rather than directly to customers.

Compared to B2C marketing, B2B marketing is more challenging because several things are at stake. For one thing, you need to take account of stakeholders and involve them at every step of the decision making process. These are complex relationships with the average B2B purchase involving 3 to 5 decision makers.

In other words, you need to create content that can speak to both decision makers and influencers who actually buy your offerings. For that to be possible, you need to forge business relationships that can last for enough years to make a positive difference in terms of gains.

Here are some aspects that can help you craft a marketing strategy that your business minded audience can respond to and engage with you:

Build Personal Customer Relations

The main focus of your B2B marketing efforts should be to forge long term relationships that can drive business growth especially during the purchasing cycle. Remember, you are selling to businesses. These can be anything from wholesalers and distributors to suppliers who are selling to resellers.

Unlike a B2C setup which has to forge an emotional connection directly with customers, there is no personal emotional involvement in a B2B purchase. In other words, rather than researching how your inventory can make their life better, you have to focus on understanding corporate buyers and their role in their organization's infrastructure.

This type of marketing focuses not on the people who use the products, but how they can save a distributor time, money, and resources. In simpler terms, what is the return on investment (ROI) they can benefit from by purchasing from you?

Let's use a simple example to understand this. Say you want to sell software to a business that will save time and money in the long run. If the tool can be used across different departments, it will be a significant purchase for the organization.

Naturally, the people who will ultimately use the product will need convincing to invest in it. Unlike customers who have no business experience, they will need referrals from companies that used it, detailed demonstrations and trial periods before they will be willing to make a serious commitment.

Speak Their Language

B2B customers are more likely to purchase services and products from companies or experts who understand their processes, the terminologies they use and the decisions they make during decision making processes. Naturally, if you want to make them understand where you are coming from, you need to speak their language by using their perspective as a guide.

For example, say you want to sell Managed WordPress hosting services for $20 a month to a company that sells apparel online. Fluffy content will only backfire here because unlike an online apparel store, your customers cannot be convinced to make any impulsive purchasing decision.

Your copy should focus on taking that emotion away from their decision and build confidence in the potential client. Telling them to "Buy this web hosting solution to increase your traffic" will leave them hanging because that type of content doesn't come with a payload. How can your solutions reduce their workload? How can it make their clients happy?

Here is a simple example of how BlueHost tackles queries like these beautifully. Just take a look at their WordPress Hosting page:

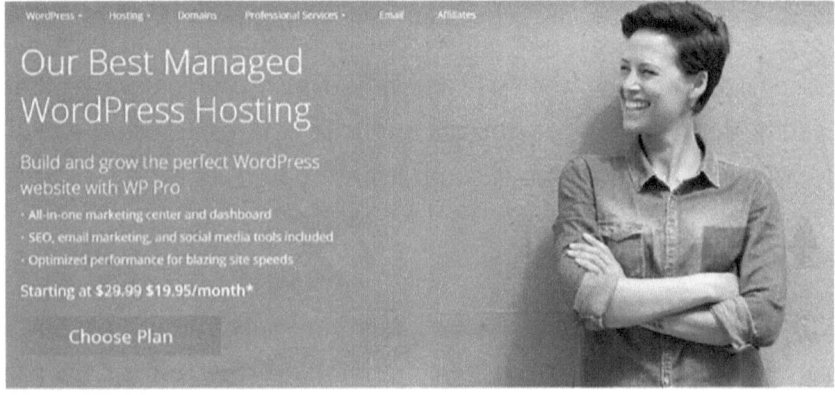

As you can see the copy is not only short and to the point, it uses terminologies that will make an IT manager sit up and take notice. After all, they are the ones who are in charge of making the purchasing decision for the web hosting service to improve overall business performance.

To ensure they make an informed decision that will benefit them and their organization in the long run, your copy has to reference their needs.

Create Focused and Personalized Websites

There is a clear difference between the personalization level you will need to attain on a B2B website compared to a B2C website. For one thing, the latter has more opportunities to personalize their content because they have far more to offer and interaction points to track in comparison.

Think about it. All they need to do is look up a customer's shopping history or track their activities using cookies to get the information they need to make targeted marketing decisions.

For example, if they see that a consumer spends more time on a specific jacket on their webpage, they will send targeted ads their way which will pop up on their browser even if they are on another website.

This strategy will not work for a B2B setup because their audience will be searching for hyper-specific content. If they land on your home page and see every webpage they viewed as ads on there, they are business and tech savvy enough to figure out that their online activities are being tracked. While this may not be taken personally, navigating through the clutter will frustrate them enough to make them switch to a competitor who has a cleaner website.

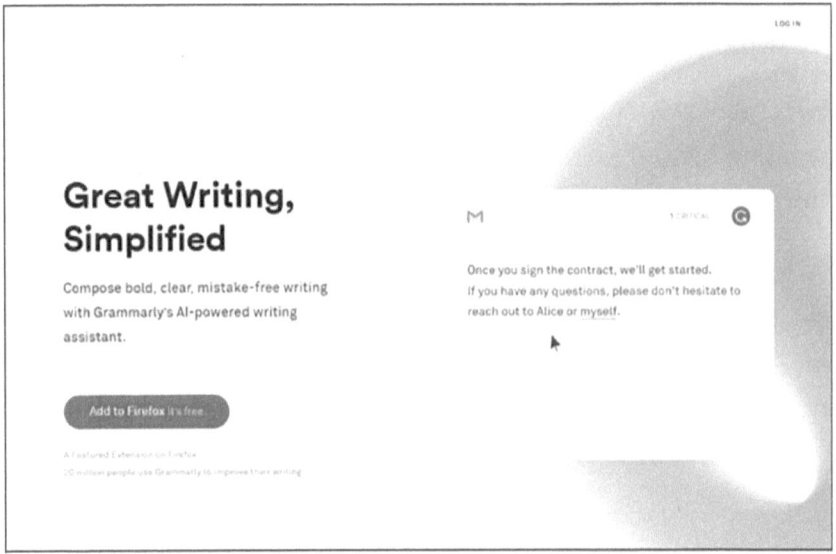

Your aim should be to connect with business minded audiences in their own element to convince them you possess solutions to their problems that they cannot do without. Grammarly is a great example of a B2B website that combines minimalism and animation to engage site visitors right from the first visit.

As you can see, the design has a simple CTA which lets visitors know in no uncertain terms what they can gain from the service. Plus, it goes the extra mile by providing examples of how

Grammarly can save them time by correcting content mistakes on the go.

Nurture your Leads

Additionally, the personalization on a B2B website is more individualistic. Unlike a B2C website in which you just need to click on a product and buy it in a few steps, you need to follow several steps to finalize a purchase for a B2B product or service.

In its simplest terms, the process can involve a form that interested parties may need to fill out, calls they need to make to sales representatives to discuss packages or discounts and finally, a contract they may need to sign to finalize their purchase.

The aim should be to nurture each lead till it converts into the aim of any B2B business. This is where informative assets can prove invaluable. By providing in depth information on services or products that a business or a department in a specific company may find useful the website should contain more than just reviews. It should contain tutorials, comparative blogs and other factual data that can trigger a quick buying decision.

Some of the elements that you should focus on include:

Explainer Videos and Demos

Videos create more brand awareness if they are relevant, informative and engaging. We aren't talking about peppy product descriptions that are narrated by overzealous hosts here. Even a simple video tutorial that shows you using software you are selling with a step by step narration can be enough to convert leads into sales.

Live Webinars

These are live events that you can stream on your website to increase brand engagement and give potential customers a unique look into the company itself. For example, you can create a video series that details special promotions or new offerings that the organization is about to introduce.

To make this really beneficial, only allow those people who sign up for a newsletter or your email list access to the webinars. This will do two things – it will make your leads feel extra special and two, it will give you precious contact details you can use to tweak your marketing strategy.

Provide Links to Download EBooks

Well researched eBooks can help you show leads how serious the business is when it comes to researching and developing their offerings. Unlike blogs which only offer snapshot information, the amount of content you can fill in a book is limited only by product and service specifications.

These can promise your leads an insider and in-depth look at what they can get from the business. This can be anything from a guide book that breaks down the benefits of technical SEO (for SEO services), a step by step tutorial that shows how a web designer creates a website from scratch (for a web design service) or anything that compels a lead to click on that download link.

Video Blogs

Video blogs offer viewers an immersive learning experience that a simple blog can fall short of. That's because they can allow you to sell not only a new product, but also yourself. By showcasing your authentic self to the masses rather than a sales representative, you can connect with potential customers on a personal level.

Just make sure that you remain true to your offerings by talking about their selling points. Plus, show that you care about your clients and how your business can answer real issues they face every day. Choose topics from your target industry and how your products matter.

Web Commercials

This is the ideal way to attract audiences on different platforms. Whether you distribute brand videos, creative commercials or small product videos online, all of them have a shared purpose – to get your business as much exposure as possible and to drive action. The more ad content you have online, the higher your chances of getting noticed.

The market is saturated with as it is. The best way you can stand out is by creating content that resonates with your audience. For instance, if you are selling customized mugs, create small videos showing how they are made keeping a client's expectations in mind.

Conclusion

"Do the difficult things while they are easy and do the great things while they are small. A journey of a thousand miles begins with a single step."

-Lao Tzu-

So, there you have it. This is just the start on how you can get around the marketing world if you, like me, have the courage to take your future into your own hands. The first thing you need to do is to look within yourself and categorize your strengths from your weaknesses. After all, if you don't know yourself intimately, how can you figure out the difference between your customers' wants and their needs?

This will require sacrifices that you think you may not be able to give. If you baulk at the first hurdle, you will never be able to realize your dreams of independence and growth. How long are you going to stay in your parent's basement dreaming dreams that will remain unfulfilled?

Use this book not just as a guide that can lead you to business and marketing success, but as a treatise that can help you realize your true potential. The only one standing in the path to your success is you.